THE
ABIDING LIFE

THE ABIDING LIFE

A BOOK ABOUT JOHN 15

Josh Houston

Editing by Lily Lee
Cover Design © 2022 by Amanda Houston
Diagrams © 2017 by Jeremy Pedron

ISBN: 197447433X
ISBN-13: 9781974474332

To Amanda,
the brightest soul I know.

CONTENTS

FOREWORD

-BY BILL DOGTEROM-

They have spent the best years of their lives learning to follow him. Some from the very beginning, still damp from the waters of baptism, hearing the stunning witness of John's prophetic voice. They have watched as he transformed water into an overabundance of wine, overwhelming the small village of Cana with the outrageous generosity of the life and joy of the dawning age. Some of them overheard the conversation as Jesus took a visiting member of the Council to school on the nature of the life to come. Early on, they had gotten used to his forays into the social borderlands – sitting as he did with a Samaritan woman of suspicious character just outside her village. And the healings! Who could forget the gratitude of the royal official – and the ingratitude of the porch dweller near the pool? Or the saddened anger on dis-play as he signaled the end of what the temple-centered worship had become? Or the leftovers from a few loaves and fish – or the I Am coming to them across a darkened, stormy sea? The tensions with the Jewish leaders, threatening to boil over with the raising of Lazarus (the raising of Lazarus!!), brought them to this Passover moment. They must have been able to sense the pressure of this night.

Dr. Samuel Johnson is quoted as saying, "…when a man knows he is to be hanged in a fortnight, it concentrates his mind wonderfully." The point being, of course, that approaching death gives a sharpness, a focus, to thought. It is not hard to think that something like that might be at work in the gospel of John, where he devotes almost a quarter of his gospel to the last words of Jesus. John is a master of concentrated time, leading his readers through moments into which eternity breaks in, as he tells the most important story in human history; roughly the first half of the gospel is devoted to the approximately three years of Jesus' public ministry, leaving the last half to focus on the last seven days, and the last quarter to cover the final twenty-four hours of Jesus' earthly life. John is laser focused on these moments, taking them slowly, expanding and circling around the narrative to make sure nothing is missed. Throughout, it becomes crystal clear that Jesus is not anxious about his own future. He knows who he is; he knows where he came from; he knows where he is going. And is supremely confident in that. Rather, his concern is for his friends, his disciples – those to whom he will hand off his plan to save the world.

The squabbling over position, characteristic throughout their time with him, continued as they made their way into dinner. So he took the place of the lowliest servant, washing their feet himself – and inviting them to love one another – and him – enough to follow his example. They were afraid and uncertain. So he promised them that he would return, and that, in the meantime, the Holy Spirit would come to help them as he had. The challenge was to remember, in a swirl of confusion and doubt and uncertainty regarding the truth of who he was, that the strategy was to follow in his way – knowing that the truth would emerge as they did so. Of primary concern to him was that they follow in his way of love – especially for one another. They are the core of a new community, defined by love. It was – is – essential that his disciples model the radical and powerful nature of that self-sacrificing love. It is the only hope for the world.

John ends his recording of Jesus' last will and testament by giving his readers a glimpse into the heart of Jesus as He prays. Moments before his arrest, his mind is focused on his disciples – and on those who would become his disciples as a result of their witness. His prayer, at the end, is that they – we – would love one another. That we who had been on the receiving end of undeserved love would, in turn, love one another in that same way. That would be the witness to a watching world – our love for one another, manifest in unity, would be incontrovertible evidence that he had, in fact, come from the Father, that he was Messiah, the son of God.

In between his last words to the disciples in the upper room, and on the way to the last words about his disciples to his Father in prayer, right in the middle of these final chapters, Jesus spoke about their identity in Him. And how not to get lost in the dark days that lay ahead for them. Chapter fifteen is the centerpiece, the piece that holds the rest together. And it is this that my former student, and now my friend and teacher, Josh Houston, considers in this series of reflections.

The seed that has germinated into this book was planted in an early conversation we had over coffee (what else?). The privilege of meeting with students outside of the classroom is one of the main reasons that I love to teach. Conversations range far and wide, depending on their interests and openness, and my ability to keep up. Every once in a while, those early conversations open up into a longer, ongoing dialogue leading to friendship. Such is the case with Josh. Early on, it became clear that he had a curiosity and capacity that stretched beyond the moment and pressed into the depths – past "how" and "what," towards "why" and "who."

Challenged to sit reflectively in John 15 for a few weeks as a way of reframing what success might look like in ministry – or life, for that matter, Josh started to pull on threads that led to other threads. It was not long before this chapter lay in bits and pieces all over the floor of his mind – only to be assembled and reassembled into new meanings and implications completely in keeping with the abiding life. Because life has a way of both shaking and stirring those who are paying attention, it will not be long before you realize that pain forces different pathways. And then those pathways, explored, lead to new vistas of understanding. Jesus is clearly aware of this as he speaks – and it is reflected in Josh's journey.

This is the fruit of faith-full, soul-full, reflective, prayer-full, scholarship. And, in typical fashion for him, always with a practical, pastoral, lens. He has taken his discoveries and led others under his care into their depths. And now, in this book, he does the same for his readers. Josh has not merely written this book – he has lived this chapter. If we live attentive to what he writes, we have the opportunity to learn of Jesus – to explore his love, complete his joy, receive the gift of his peace. Nothing more could be asked of a book.

PREFACE

WHY READ THIS BOOK?
-A NOTE FROM THE AUTHOR-

"Abide in me." The instruction Christ gave to those coura-geous enough to follow. Simply put, abiding is the defin-ing trait of a disciple, and it's what this book is all about. Candidly, I wrote the book I wish someone gave me when I started taking this whole "Jesus" thing seriously. It's filled with insights and perspectives that have helped me actually begin living the life we as Christians like to talk about, but often feel is unattainable.

You may understand the dilemma yourself. Jesus spoke about salvation. Not just getting to heaven, but newness of life here on this side of eternity. Life that stands beyond the reach of sin; life capable of carrying true peace and full joy beyond a moment or season. Abundant life is what he liked to call it. But it almost sounds too good to be true, right?

I've been in the church world my entire life and am quite famil-iar with what we refer to as "professional Christianity." Learning the right answers is easy, but for a large chunk of the western Church, there seems to be a disconnect between what they say they believe, and how they feel and behave regarding those beliefs.

Abundant life, joy, trust in God, faith that moves mountains... is this really possible?

We talk about Christ freeing us from sin, fear, and stress, but how many people do you know truly demonstrate a life lived in this freedom? Maybe you've been taught to take off the old self and put on the new self, but then nothing changes. What does that even mean anyway? Maybe you've said a prayer of faith in Christ, you've been baptized, and have even engaged in a flourishing church community, yet the life you heard possible seems not entirely possible, for you at least.

But who wants to admit that, right? "I'm basing my entire life and eternity off truth that isn't quite true for me." While this sounds like an unfortunate reality, many genuine-hearted, well-intentioned Christians are living it every day. Maybe you are, too.

So how do we move from abundant life in theory to abundant life in practice? From the truth found in the Bible, to the truth of the Bible found in me? What's missing? My hypothesis: the abiding life. People miss life change because their lives are not aligned with God's. Whether intentionally or not, many of us have figured out how to live the oxymoron of following Jesus on our own terms, which frankly is not possible. God desires union with us, and this happens through a life committed to abiding.

I think back to a lakeside afternoon I spent with God. After a fair amount of quiet inactivity, a canoe came into view, carrying what appeared to be a mother and daughter. I watched as the mother rowed elegantly in the back, steering the boat in the direction she wanted it to go. The young daughter sat in the front, arbitrarily slapping her paddle at the water. Humorously enough, more than half the time she splashed water forward and sideways, making it more difficult for the mother to point the canoe in the right direction. I do that a lot!

In that moment I realized how this little girl's rowing often resembled my own relationship with Jesus. I watched her, intently

At one point ignorance is no longer bliss, its ignorance.

striving to move the canoe, thinking her paddling was making significant impacts on the direction. And to some extent, it was true: her paddling often pushed the canoe in the wrong direction. She had no idea what she was doing, and showed no attempt to line up her paddling with the one actually in charge of the canoe's direction.

I regularly wind up in conversation with Christians who want their lives to move in the "right direction," endeavoring to make wise decisions, but then leave out the principal catalyst for rowing in the "correct direction:" abiding. Abiding is what many disregard. Abiding is specifically what lines our hearts up with God's so that our well-intentioned and determined efforts are not in vain.

Why read this book? Because this book is all about abiding. And without taking seriously the instruction of Jesus to abide in him, your life will be lived in friction, maybe even opposition to the one directing your life. Without abiding, your life cannot function at full capacity. Without abiding, it is impossible to live out your intended design.

When the Church is functioning the way Christ designed it, the world flourishes. Relationships, organizations, systems, power... they teem with life when the Church is working. And in order for the Church to function properly, it must be filled with Christians tenaciously committed to the abiding life. The opposite is true as well though. Christians caught up in religious activity without devoting themselves to abiding in Christ will produce relational, organizational, systemic, and power breakdown in all of life. Plainly, life apart from abiding is dysfunctional; it simply does not work.

While God is sovereign, for some reason he gave his Church the distinct honor of representing him on earth for the time being. Christ's Church has been called and commissioned as his ambassadors, on mission to demonstrate his unwavering commitment to humanity. The crucial element frequently left out of the conversation, however, is that the Church's representation of Christ will be

Am I stunting my growth? Am I keeping myself from an abundant life because I choose ignorance. What if I abide?

in direct relation to how well she has learned to abide in him, and the abiding life only happens by way of intentionality. We rarely drift into health and wellbeing. Drifting nearly always draws us in the direction of dysfunction and un-health. Abiding is a commitment to a lifestyle, a new paradigm, and this book is purposed to set you up for becoming an intentional and disciplined abider.

In the following chapters I'll touch on choosing Christ as your vine, what it practically means to abide in Christ on a daily basis, our intended relationship with fruit, our response to pruning, how to get what we want in prayer, the necessity of love, and joy beyond our circumstances.

Abundant and joy-filled life is in fact possible when we do what Jesus asks. He knows how to change the world, and astonishingly he calls us to be part of that change. If we will allow God to change our hearts, he will change the world through us. The abiding life is how we do it.

It's my hope that these pages will fill your hearts with faith, and instill in you a desire to surrender the caverns of your soul to Christ. I have prayed long and hard that this book would wonderfully wreck your life. My prayer over you as you sift through the pages awaiting is one prayed over Brennan Manning many years ago by his spiritual director, Larry Hine: "May all your expectations be frustrated, may all your plans be thwarted, may all your desires be withered into nothingness, that you may experience the powerlessness and poverty of a child, and sing and dance in the love of God who is the Father, Son, and Spirit."

XVI

ACKNOWLEDGMENTS

Thanks to all who helped make this project a reality:

Amanda - *you're my favorite*

Dad and Ma - *everything I am and have is a consequence of your faithfulness*

Gordie, Scotty, and Zoomp - *a cord of four strands is not quickly broken*

Bill - *you taught me how to sit at the feet of Jesus*

Nate - *this book would not be if not for our conversation on that plane ride*

Lily - *my rock star editor, you pulled no punches*

"I am the true vine, and My Father is the vinedresser.
Every branch in Me that does not bear fruit He takes away;
and every branch that bears fruit,
He prunes it so that it may bear more fruit.
You are already clean because of the word
which I have spoken to you. Abide in Me, and I in you.
As the branch cannot bear fruit of itself
unless it abides in the vine,
so neither can you unless you abide in Me.
I am the vine, you are the branches;
he who abides in Me and I in him, he bears much fruit,
for apart from Me you can do nothing.
If anyone does not abide in Me, he is thrown away as a branch
and dries up; and they gather them,
and cast them into the fire and they are burned.
If you abide in Me, and My words abide in you,
ask whatever you wish and it will be done for you.
My Father is glorified by this, that you bear much fruit,
and so prove to be My disciples.
Just as the Father has loved Me,
I have also loved you; abide in My love.
If you keep My commandments, you will abide in My love;
just as I have kept My Father's commandments
and abide in His love.
These things I have spoken to you
so that My joy may be in you,
and that your joy may be made full."
JOHN 15:1-11 (NASB)

CHAPTER 1.1

ABIDE

-CHOOSE YOUR VINE-

> *"I am the true vine, and my Father is the vinedresser...*
> *Abide in Me, and I in you.*
> *As the branch cannot bear fruit of itself*
> *unless it abides in the vine,*
> *so neither can you unless you abide in Me."*
> **JOHN 15:1, 4**

> *"Christian spirituality, simply put,*
> *is God's passionate embrace of us,*
> *and our passionate embrace of God."[1]*
> **ROBERT E. WEBBER**

Glass Slippers

I remember the days when I read Scripture without context. All verses existed in and of themselves. Authorship, location, time, culture, audience... none of these mattered regarding my reading of God's Word because I believed the Spirit could teach me

---

1 Robert E. Webber, *The Divine Embrace: Recovering the Passionate Spiritual Life*, 16.

whatever he wanted as long as I was open to it. Those were the days when ignorance was bliss. Now ignorance is just ignorant.

Although I still believe the Spirit gives insight into his Word for those willing to listen, I don't know an individual to whom God has taught first-century culture or Koine Greek. What I'm getting at here is that we must find a healthy balance of learning some background, culture, and context, mixed with a genuine humility of knowing there will be things into which God speaks that no teacher or book could ever explain. When it comes to encountering God in Scripture, our approach should not be study *or* inspiration; it must be *both-and*.

To start, culture and context are fundamental for reading Scripture, because in the words of a close friend of mine, "Scripture is full of glass slippers." To explain, when you hear the words "glass slipper," what immediately comes to mind? Cinderella, right? Just the mention of those two words may bring a plethora of images, characters, story, feelings, and memories. In a similar way, the writers of Scripture had their own "glass slippers." The mere reference of a town, number, or image flooded the ancient mind with ideas, stories, feelings, and memories. Understanding culture and context invites today's readers, at least partially, into recognizing the common knowledge available to the original readers or hearers of the text.

That being said, I don't plan to swing to the end of the spectrum, providing an exhaustive study or commentary for John 15. This work is not intended to be scholarly in nature. Instead, my purpose is to invite you, the reader, into the marvelous reality of intimacy with Jesus. I plan to then provide a basic background and contextual foundation for what we encounter in John 15, and use that as a launch pad into what it practically means to live it out. I find that even a little cultural understanding can greatly impact a simple reading of Scripture, bringing light and clarity in a way we didn't know was possible.

A Little Context

In chapter 15 of John's gospel, we find Jesus in conversation with the remaining eleven disciples. They had just celebrated the Passover and were on the trail leading into the Kidron Valley and up the slope of the Mount of Olives to the Garden of Gethsemane. Many scholars agree the conversation started by Jesus in chapter 15 was far from random; it was likely an opportunity for teaching based off their surroundings, which was quite consistent with Jesus's teaching style- one that ebbed and flowed with situations, people, and landscape, often welcoming interruptions. He seems to have been unfailingly content with any situation presenting itself, knowing he could in some way use it as a teaching point for his disciples.

As they walked along the trail, Jesus and his disciples would have passed through the vineyards surrounding the city. I like to picture Jesus and his friends wandering through the vineyards, taking in the sights and smells of the freshly pruned grapevines. And as they passed by the front of the temple, Jesus likely began his teaching on abiding.

Why here though? Why this conversation now? The answer would have been quite obvious to the average first-century Jew, but for us, context is crucial. Displayed on the front of the temple was a golden vine with hanging grape clusters- a sight Josephus called a marvel of size and artistry. The vine was also used to represent Jerusalem on coins made during the first Jewish revolt, and was a familiar Old Testament image for the nation of Israel as expressed through the psalmists, Isaiah, and Jeremiah. It can be helpful to think of it this way: much like a country's flag being waved, the vine was clearly a symbol; even more so, a national emblem for Israel.

In this light, Jesus begins his teaching to the disciples with an extraordinary notion: (my translation) "So you know how Israel is illustrated as the vine? Well, I'd like to present an alternate paradigm for you: I am the Vine; the only authentic and genuine Vine at that, and I stand in sharp contrast to the symbol Israel represents. I am the fulfillment of everything suggested and implied in that symbol. I am the true Vine; the only Vine."

Once again Jesus takes something common and well understood by his friends and flips it on its head. What we must understand here is that his claim had significant consequences for his listeners. By taking the image of Israel and applying it to himself, Jesus asks his friends to no longer identify themselves by their nationality- a ludicrous notion in his day. His desire was that the identification of all people with the nation of Israel would be replaced by their identification with him.

This discussion would have been truly paradigm shifting for the disciples, had they understood it at the time. More than a mere conversation about a symbol, it was one of identity.

Identity

Jesus states rather plainly the characters involved in his teaching: he is the true vine, his Father is the vinedresser, and his followers are the branches. Although Jesus is clearly speaking to his disciples here, this simple metaphor conveys substantial implications for us today as well.

Firstly, I want to point out that Jesus identifies himself as the *true* vine. He doesn't claim to be the only option; he says he is the correct one. Which means his followers are given the freedom to identify with other vines that will not produce the same fruit-namely, lasting fruit. No doubt, this conversation would have been thought provoking for the disciples. Jesus's assertion: (my translation, once more) "Choose your vine, and choose it wisely, because the fruit of your life will be dependent upon who or what is your source." In other words, you will bear fruit. That is not in question. What is in question is what kind of fruit you will bear, and that will be determined by what vine you choose to abide in.

Additionally, the decision the disciples would make regarding their vine would be dependent on who they believed Jesus to be. Jesus once asked Peter a question that would determine his destiny: "Who do you say that I am?" Remarkably, both the relevance and consequence of this question have changed little. Today Jesus asks us the same question. Do not be mistaken, though; he does not ask this question to the Church at large. He does not ask who your pastor, best friend, grandmother, or favorite author says he is. Jesus asks you today: "Who do *you* say that I am?" And your answer to this question will ultimately impact your decision in choosing or denying Jesus as your vine.

But in a real sense, what does choosing Jesus as our vine actually mean? In short, it means he becomes our priority in life. I once read an article by Greg McKeown entitled: *There Can Only Be One No. 1: The Best-Kept Secret About Priorities.* This is what he writes:

> "When the word 'priority' came into the English language in the 1400s, it only existed in the singular form. It meant the very first or prior thing. It stayed singular for the next five hundred years. Only in the 1900s did we pluralize the term and start talking about 'priorities.' Illogically, we reasoned that by changing the word we could bend reality. Somehow we thought that by pluralizing the word we would now be able to have multiple 'first' things."

In line with Mckeown's thoughts, Jesus cannot share the number one spot with the other most important things. Our lives are either about Jesus, or they're not. Additionally, there are macro and microelements to this notion. In a macro sense, Jesus must become the purpose of our lives, but in a micro sense, the abiding life invites Jesus to become our priority in every decision, every moment, every day.

Abiding draws itself into the mundane, just as much as the "religious." Riding a bicycle, preparing a meal, cleaning the bathroom... every moment carries capacity to be an abiding moment. Every moment has potential to be holy. The abiding life stirs you to choose Jesus as your vine, as best you can, making him your priority in every facet of life, and then asking him for help to continue doing so.

Jesus also communicates that if his followers would choose him as their vine, his Father *must* be their vinedresser. The implications here are profound. As vinedresser, the Father would get the final say on what happens in their lives. He chooses what stays and what gets pruned off. Ultimately he decides the direction of the vine's growth, which generates consequences to the branch's growth.

But who cares, right? What difference is it to us that Jesus wanted his followers to be identified solely in him and give control of their lives to the Father? I know Christians who, for the most part, identify as Christian and believe God is in control of their lives. The problem, however, comes when they delve into how much of their identity is rooted in Christ, and how much control of their lives has been given to the Father.

Claiming our identity is rooted in God takes little effort. Confessing to God we give him control of our lives, calling him "Lord," is easy. The waters get murky, however, when we examine the "how?" and "how much?" questions. Practically, how are we day-to-day rooting our identities in Christ? How are we giving control of the real situations in our lives over to the Father? Christians who've been around the Church block a time or two know the right answers, but have we allowed the learned, theoretical truths to saturate our hearts enough to change the way we act and think when we find ourselves in darker moments?

Unfortunately this is not an attractive message in our culture. "Give up the right to be in control of my life to the Father of some Rabbi they called Jesus?" While an exceptionally confrontational message, there's also a subtle beauty to this charge. When Jesus becomes my center, when the Father gets command of my life, I become nothing more and nothing less than what I was designed to be: a branch. And the potent truth of my branch-ness delicately transforms my dysfunction. In time, my identity as a branch sifts through fear, anxiety, and stress, making way for full joy.

Robert Mulholland Jr. writes that when we seek to root our being in something other than God, we are a false self.[2] *Essentially, we have no shot at fulfilling the purpose of our lives if we reject rooting ourselves in the being that calls us to that purpose.* At a fundamental level, we must begin to align our lives with the one directing the vine if we hope to experience any degree of a joy-filled life.

Furthermore, while purpose and joy are qualities after which to be sought, a life of abiding in Christ offers far more. More than a mere recommendation for a happy life, abiding is an invitation into life-giving relationship with the Inventor of the universe. Personally, I savor how Jesus discloses the Father's true feelings about us in Scripture. As we turn the pages of the gospels, we soon discover that the people Jesus encounters- the prostitutes, tax collectors, lepers, children, crowds, and his disciples- they are you and I. The love, compassion, and grace he offered them, he offers us today. This is the life into which he invites us. The abiding life.

I want to suggest that God does not love you just because, theologically, he has to. God's love for you is a daily, chosen love. In fact, he loves you more than you have the capacity to comprehend or appreciate, but he is also extremely fond of you. I believe he is thoroughly "in like" with you. The command to abide is instruction to define yourself as one radically beloved of God, fixed into the vine. The vinedresser's love for you and his thoughts toward you constitute your worth. It is an offer to accept your acceptance; to let his love for you become the absolute meaning of your life.

---

2 M. Robert Mulholland Jr., *The Deeper Journey: the Spirituality of Discovering Your True Self*, 45.

In the end, it becomes a matter of accepting your true identity, because every other identity is merely an illusion overpromising what it will in time, under-deliver.

This is the beginning of the way of Jesus; our commencement into the abiding life. And it arises from this first decision. Choose your vine.

CHAPTER 1.2

ABIDE

-CHOOSING THE ABIDING LIFE-

"I am the true vine, and my Father is the vinedresser...
Abide in Me, and I in you.
As the branch cannot bear fruit of itself
unless it abides in the vine,
so neither can you unless you abide in Me."
JOHN 15:1, 4

"Christian spirituality, simply put,
is God's passionate embrace of us,
and our passionate embrace of God."[3]
ROBERT E. WEBBER

Transitioning from Choosing the Vine to Abiding in the Vine

So we've made the decision to choose Jesus as our vine, but now what? What does it mean to practically and daily abide in him? Without a plan, good intentions leak. Without aiming in a specific direction, eventually we find ourselves in no better

---

3 Robert E. Webber, *The Divine Embrace: Recovering the Passionate Spiritual Life*, 16.

shape than someone who wants to be healthy but has failed to look into dietary change and workout routines. Changing our intentions is a great start, but then we need to move beyond intention into a commitment to do something about the way we're living.

Little Houdini

As a child I took up the art of illusion and misdirection- a.k.a. magic tricks. I remember at the age of five or six, learning my first trick from the rabbit on a Winnie the Pooh kids show. The fact that this little trick fooled my mom instantly hooked me. I began saving for and buying bigger and better magic tricks, starting with the cheap ones you find at toy stores, and eventually moved on to more difficult and expensive tricks only found at magic shops or online.

Now, although all magic can be entertaining and fun, what I enjoy most are card tricks. I consider myself more of a *cardician* who has delved into the world of magic than I am a magician in the greater sense of the word. I find something truly special in being handed a deck of cards and being able to bring a sense of wonder to a room.

This timeless art form has become one of my all-time favorite hobbies. To my own intrigue, however, I have discovered while performing magic for all age groups, I usually encounter at least one person in the group that comes up afterwards with a quiet, "Can you tell me how you did the one with the queens?" Usually this person wants to know how I did the trick so he can go impress his friends with it. The problem is that while he wants to know the secret for the purpose of "becoming a magician too," I often get approached regarding my most difficult tricks. These are the tricks I literally spent hours in front of a mirror perfecting. Unfortunately in some of my beginner years, my kind heart would give in to the person genuinely wanting to know the secret so he or she might become a future colleague of mine. Consequently, some of my favorite tricks were exposed due to the impatience of the person wanting to impress onlookers with my trick, yet not having the discipline to practice it until it was more than ready to be performed. Today if I ever teach someone a trick, I have a two-point checklist before they can perform the trick in front of anyone: do it in front of a mirror until you can fool yourself, and then do it in front of me.

The point I hope to make here is this: *a person who expects to perform difficult card tricks without the discipline and preparation it takes to perform them with precision, is no less ridiculous than a branch that expects to bear healthy fruit without the discipline and preparation it takes to abide in the vine.*

Abiding is not figured out in a day because someone teaches you about it in a class, conversation, or Bible study. It is not something you become proficient in because a sermon or book gave you three points to becoming an abider- not even this book. Abiding is a discipline learned over a lifetime. It is a journey, a pilgrimage into union with Christ that requires our blood, sweat, and tears. The abiding life demands unbending fortitude, and our commitment to it will be tested again and again.

To be direct though, I find a difficulty in this word "abide" in that it's not often practically spoken of. It would, therefore, do you no good if I wrote a book about John 15 without diving into the discipline of abiding. To prelude this, in no way am I proposing to have cornered the market on abiding. I simply have read much, have asked a lot of questions to spiritual mentors and pastors, and have encountered God myself, and I believe in one way or another what I've learned can help you as you learn to better abide as well.

Abide In Me

As explained earlier, we are merely branches. Whether we choose to acknowledge it yet or not, this is our identity. When we sit with the nature of our branch-ness, we understand at a fundamental level that we were created to abide and bear fruit. The purpose of a branch on a fruit-bearing tree or plant is fruit production. Vinedressers do not cultivate grape vines to admire their pretty leaves. While hills and fields of grapevines are a lovely sight, vinedressers take the trouble to plant, water, and tend the vines so fruit and/or wine can be enjoyed.

Jesus's words were simple and precise: "Abide in me." But he also informed his disciples that their ability to bear fruit without abiding in him would be as possible as a branch bearing fruit without its vine. In other words, you will not catch a branch growing legs and running away from its source- not if it wants to bear fruit. In short, *bearing lasting fruit is impossible without abiding, but is the inevitable result of an abiding life*. Abiding is the key to fruit. The quality and quantity of the fruit will differ from branch to branch, but fruit will yield nonetheless.

We'll touch on fruit in the next chapter. For now, we should sit with the notion that if we don't choose the abiding life, bearing Kingdom fruit will prove to be an impossibility for us.

CHAPTER 1.3

ABIDE

-DEFINING "ABIDE"-

> *"I am the true vine, and my Father is the vinedresser...*
> *Abide in Me, and I in you.*
> *As the branch cannot bear fruit of itself*
> *unless it abides in the vine,*
> *so neither can you unless you abide in Me."*
> **JOHN 15:1, 4**

> *"Christian spirituality, simply put,*
> *is God's passionate embrace of us,*
> *and our passionate embrace of God."[4]*
> ROBERT E. WEBBER

Defining "Abide"

I n a fun way, friends of mine mock me regarding how consistently I reference John 15. Thanks to Bill Dogterom, who has been a friend, mentor, and pastor to me for many years, John 15 has become my filter for life. We have circled abiding for years,

---

4 Robert E. Webber, *The Divine Embrace: Recovering the Passionate Spiritual Life*, 16.

and I now find it difficult not to bring it up in conversation with others. Beyond merely bringing it up in conversation, however, I attempt to put handles on it. How can I actually grab hold of this teaching?

The truth is, we all grapple with difficult situations and frustrating people, but it is far too easy as a pastor to tell someone stressing about life, "Just abide. God will take care of it all." Candidly, this is irresponsible. Beyond offering a little hope, you can't do much with, "Just abide. God will take care of it all."

So what does the abiding life look like? How can we know what to shoot for? Unfortunately, the term can prove to be quite ambiguous when we talk about it. While we may recognize when we're in the presence of one who abides, few of us have taken the time to carefully break down its primary components. Yet defining precisely what we're shooting for is a critical first step if we hope to take John 15 seriously.

When I first committed my heart to the abiding life, I soon realized I had no way to measure it. And when I looked for an agreed upon understanding of abiding, I found myself even more confused. If you ask a hundred different pastors, teachers, and Bible scholars what Jesus meant when he commanded his followers to abide, you'll probably receive a hundred different answers.

So I figured I'd start simple. In classic pastor form, I looked at Merriam-Webster's definition for abide: *to bear patiently; to endure or remain fixed without yielding; to await; to accept without obligation.* While this suffices as a starting point, I knew in the long run it would probably be a little too general.

Eventually, after much research and conversation, including conversation with the Holy Spirit, I landed on three necessary minimums that appear to cover most of what I discovered and holistically defined what I was looking for. They form my working definition of the abiding life. Your list for abiding may differ, but this three-fold grid is a good place to start:

1. Identity in Jesus
2. Intimacy with Jesus
3. Obedience to Jesus

Identity In Jesus

First and foremost, the abiding life means rooting identity in Jesus. *Either your lifestyle and life roles will form your identity, or your lifestyle and life roles will be formed by your identity.* One will be the driving force behind the other, and if we don't get it right on the front side, we end up with a lot to clean up later.

Abiding nudges you to question where you find and root your identity. Is it in your job as the custodian, pediatrician, accountant, or visual effects artist? Is it in your familial role as the father, grandmother, uncle, or daughter? Is it in your sexual orientation, in what local church you attend, the color of your collar, the color of your skin, your education, or your favorite sports team? If so, abiding for you falls short. Abiding shamelessly asserts if you root identity in anything but Jesus, he is not your source, which means the fruit of your life is not being nourished from him.

We only know who we are because we know who He is. And we can only do and be what we were designed for if we first identify who we are and Whom we are in. Furthermore, and horticulturally speaking, no fruit can be greater than the vine producing it. This illustrates wonderfully the critical nature of our identifying with and in the true vine. Without him, fruitful life is impossible.

Another element I'll add here is that in the beginning stages of rooting our identity in Christ, it may seem forced and clunky. Frankly, it's anything but natural, and it's something we have to remind ourselves regularly of. Because we have been trained for so long in finding identity elsewhere, rooting identity in Christ is a fight. Eventually, however, immersing ourselves in this reality becomes the norm rather than strained effort. Similar to learning a language, rooting identity in Christ takes time and can be frustrating because of how strange it feels, but in time it becomes natural; it becomes our first language. Eventually we don't have to think about thinking about it. We don't have to think about speaking, or even dreaming about it. It will have become the language of our souls. First and foremost, identity in Jesus.

Intimacy with Jesus

Secondly, the abiding life means intimacy with Jesus. Intimacy implies close relationship: *knowing and being known by another.*

Sit with this for a second: the Being who invented strawberries desires intimacy with you. How truly remarkable. And thankfully, Jesus sets the tone for us in this. He instructs his followers to abide in him, *as he abides in them.* Jesus is not just asking us to carry the weight of intimacy. *He's asking us to model our pursuit of intimacy with him after his pursuit of intimacy with us.* The reason: a branch not intimate with its vine has no chance of fulfilling what it was destined to be or do. Even if we take fruit out of the picture for a second, without intimacy between the vine and branch, the branch dries up and dies. End of story.

I suggest taking a moment to think through how you would describe your regular, alone time with Jesus; or maybe asking yourself if you even have regular, alone time with Jesus. And avoid justifying a lack of spending time with God by thinking, "I pray throughout my day." I find this to be the classic excuse of Christians lacking regular, alone time with God. Talking to God throughout the day should be a given for Christians. We talk to Jesus. That's our baseline. But do you spend focused, uninterrupted time with your vine in a given week? If not, I'm not sure your life can be defined as an abiding one.

Let's look at it this way: let's say you asked into the health of my marriage. I reply that our relationship is exceptionally strong. You ask, "So you two go out on dates regularly?" I respond, "No, not really." You ask back, "Well, then you two must have deep conversations at home regularly, right? You talk about your passions, your fears, your dreams for the future...?" My response: "No, not really. Normally I wake up and go to work. Then I get home. I watch TV, work out a little, take a shower, and then jump into bed. But I think about my wife regularly. I even have a picture of her on my desk that I look at a few times a day. But seriously, our marriage is really healthy."

Even though you aren't in my marriage, simply by description you might disagree regarding the health of my marriage. In fact, if you were a close friend, you might even confront me about it; that I need to change my actions to line up with my intentions for my marriage.

I think many of us need to change our actions to line up with our intentions for our relationships with Jesus. Yes, relationships require time spent apart from the other. Relationships also need the social element- hanging out with another couple or even groups of people. But intimate and alone time is irreplaceable when it comes to healthy relationship, right? There's no difference with Jesus.

Many would argue they don't have enough time in the week to have routine and consistent alone time with Jesus; that they're just too busy for it. I would argue, however, the busier your week, the more essential your alone time with Jesus is that week. And I'm not talking about an hour a day here. Do you know how much ten minutes alone with Jesus every day can impact your life?

I want to bring up two factors here that come into play with the intimacy conversation: relationship with God founded on fear, and relationship with God founded on an internal sense of morality.

Firstly, having a relationship with God because you're scared to go to hell is not much of a relationship. To expound, imagine I'm walking down the street with my wife, and a beautiful woman passes by. Because I'm such an extraordinary man, I don't even give this stunning stranger a glance. I look at my wife and say, "You are exceptionally beautiful, my love." She replies back, "I'm so in love with you. You didn't even glance at that attractive, younger woman." To which I respond, "I really wanted to. In fact, I almost told her how attracted I am to her, which is quite a bit if I'm honest, but I was scared you would have smacked me." Smack to the face, right? What kind of relationship is that?

Or let's say it's my wife's birthday today, so I bought her an exquisite diamond necklace. As I present it to her she says, "Honey that was so sweet. Thank you." I reply, "You're welcome, my love, but I only did it because that's what good husbands should do, right?" Smacked again!

To further illustrate, I stumbled upon a thought-provoking term awhile back: "moralistic therapeutic deism." It describes the mindset of many Christians today. Essentially, moralistic therapeutic deists believe:

- a God exists who created and watches over human life on earth;
- God wants people to be good, nice, and fair to each other;
- a central goal of life is to be happy and to feel good about oneself;
- God does not need to be particularly involved in one's life except when he is needed to resolve a problem;
- good people go to heaven when they die.

Now, I have a hunch that the average Christian would say this doesn't accurately describe himself, yet, many go to church because they're "supposed to," and they obey God because they're frightened he will punish them. This is not descriptive of relationship- not wholesome relationship anyway.

You have been called to share intimacy with Jesus, your Creator, because of love, not because you're scared of him or because it's "the right thing to do." Intimacy founded on fear or mere obligation is actually far from intimacy. It's wise of us to dig for something more sustaining than that.

Additionally, while we may understand that we're called to intimacy with Jesus, spending time with him can be a challenging, mysterious, and trying discipline to learn. I frequently find myself in conversations with friends struggling with how to simply be with Jesus for ten minutes. Sure, it sounds easy enough, but I think all of us can acknowledge spending time with a God we cannot physically see or touch, or audibly hear, is just plain difficult. Although it may be similar to hanging out with a best friend, we have to admit it is vastly different.

In light of this, I think it appropriate to include thoughts from Gary Thomas's book, *Sacred Pathways*. His work has been exceptionally helpful for me as I've sifted through learning into intimacy with Christ.

The short version goes like this: each soul has a particular spiritual bent, an ingrained spiritual pathway by which we commune and connect with God most naturally.

Thomas breaks it up this way:

- Naturalists love God outdoors.
- Sensates love God with the senses.
- Traditionalists love God through ritual and symbol.
- Ascetics love God in solitude and simplicity.
- Activists love God through confrontation.

- Caregivers love God through loving others.
- Enthusiasts love God with mystery and celebration.
- Contemplatives love God through adoration.
- Intellectuals love God with the mind.

Now, the point here is not to limit or pigeonhole us into one "sacred pathway," but to identify how we have been uniquely wired for intimacy with God where our souls come alive to him. Understanding which sacred pathway(s) we naturally tend toward can help us to more often and readily connect with God, but also respect the ways in which those around us will connect with God as well.

The reason I bring this up is because I've counseled far too many friends who felt like their relationship with God was lacking, while people in their lives keep telling them to read more Scripture, pray more, or fast more until it gets better. Not to say we shouldn't partake in spiritual disciplines uncomfortable to us, or that we shouldn't take part in activities founded in other "sacred pathways;" they're all beneficial in some way or another. The point is that we have a more natural connection with God when we entertain our sacred pathway(s). So when you feel distant from God, when you sense that your approach to God has been blocked, I would encourage you to fall back on your sacred pathway for a season.

If you connect best with God when viewing his creation, go sit at the beach for an afternoon or sit under the stars for an evening. If you connect best with God when learning, get a new book, read some Scripture, or listen to a new podcast. If you connect best with God through caregiving, find people in need and serve them. If it's through worship music and time alone with Jesus, do that. See if that doesn't spark up your affection and passion for intimacy with Jesus. If your intimacy with Jesus is not where you want it to be, if you're having trouble getting into a groove in your time with God, go to your sweet spot.

I also want to add here some simple suggestions for alone time with God, because although you may be able to recognize your spiritual inclination (sacred pathway), figuring out how to regularly spend intimate time with Jesus can be difficult. What should that time practically look like? What actions, or non-actions, should fill that space? How often should we spend time with Jesus alone, realistically? And how much time should we spend with him during those periods of time?

I think these are honest questions, and questions many Christians are asking, so here's what I recommend: offer yourself a reachable goal. If you're not spending regular, intimate time with Jesus at all, it's not realistic to assume you will begin spending an hour a day, every day with him. People who give themselves this type of goal set themselves up for failure. It's a like a chain smoker expecting to quit tomorrow simply out of will power. While it may work for some, it won't work for most.

Similarly, a realistic approach to time with Jesus could look like selecting three to four days a week, ten to fifteen minutes on these days, and putting these days in your calendar. For example, "Monday, Wednesday, and Friday mornings at 7am, I am going to be intentionally present to Jesus for fifteen minutes, whether I feel like it or not." *Don't try to merely find time in your day for Jesus. If he is priority, make space in your calendar for him.*

Additionally, what specifically should we be doing during this time? My recommendation: don't be too rigid with it. While there may be wrong ways to hang out with Jesus, there is no right way. Here are some helpful options: fill that space with things like reading a small passage from the Word and meditating on it, active prayer (confession, petition, intercession, thanksgiving…), contemplative prayer (silence, listening, receiving, meditating on

God...)[5], journaling, other spiritual readings, admiring the stars, ocean, or paintings, or worship through song. Don't be afraid to create a regular rhythm, but don't tie yourself to it either. I would also ask Jesus what he thinks you should fill that time with. I bet he has some good ideas.

Maybe most importantly, go into that time with little to no expectation. *The goal of your intimate time with Jesus should not be to receive or gain something. The goal is to show up; to be present to Jesus.* We often spend time with God expecting him to give to us, but I'd like to suggest that sometimes God wants to receive from us as well. We shouldn't always expect him to be the giver or sacrifice-er during our time with him. Sometimes, our time with him will cost us much. If we simply show up, laying down our expectations of what will, or is supposed to happen, our time with him will never be wrong because we were with him.

And to offer hope to some readers: I am committed to the belief that God speaks to us. If we give him room and space, in time he will speak to our hearts, and we will know it was him. If God wants to speak to you, you'll know. If God wants you to know something, you will get it. I assure you, it is not too difficult for the Creator of the universe to communicate to you. Just show up with an open heart; you won't go wrong.

Lastly for this section on intimacy, I want to add that when I think of intimacy with Jesus, I think of Joshua in Scripture. Exodus 33 tells of how Moses and Joshua would meet with God in what they called the tent of meeting. Verse 11 reads: "The LORD used to speak to Moses face to face, just as a man speaks to his friend. When Moses returned to the camp, his servant

---

5 Prayer is not simply talking to God. Prayer was invented by God for humanity as a means of communication and relationship with him, which means our prayer lives should include speaking to God, making space for God to speak to us, and making space for God to simply be with us beyond words. God loves to both speak to us and hang out with us in silence, but many Christians rarely give him space or time to do either.

Joshua, the son of Nun, a young man, would not depart from the tent."

The word *linger* comes to mind here. Linger means to stay in a place longer than necessary. Joshua was a lingerer. *Abiding is learning to linger in the presence of the vine;* learning to intimately waste time with your source simply out of the love of being with him. Lingering should be a defining factor of our relationship with Jesus because with a right heart, lingering creates the environment for deeper intimacy with Jesus.

Obedience to Jesus

Thirdly, the abiding life means obedience to Jesus. Christianity is not easy but it's not complicated, either. Jesus said, "If you love me, you will keep my commands."[6] According to Jesus, we cannot claim to love him if we won't do what he tells us to.

Once again, questions like these could and should be asked: but what does that look like? How is one obedient to God? Does it just mean reading the Bible and doing whatever it says? Does it mean doing what we're informed of during our intimate time with Jesus? If that's true, what does God's voice sound like? Does it mean living out what our pastor instructs? Is it a mixture of all of these? Is there more?

These are all great questions, and in no way am I going to comprehensively explain hearing the voice of God or living an obedient life to him. Whole books have been written on obedience to the voice of God. I will, however, share a few ideas regarding obedience to God that have worked for myself and for others I've journeyed with, and I believe they are good places to start.

When it comes to obedience, I like to begin with Jesus's conversation with the woman caught in adultery. After Jesus outwitted the crowd and there's no one left holding stones, Jesus

---

6 John 14:15

communicates to the woman two life-altering statements: "I do not condemn you," and "Go and leave your life of sin."[7] Obedience first and foremost sits in the reality that we are not the sum of our accomplishments or failures. The God of the heavens condemns you not, but then asks that you change your actions. These two go hand in hand.

I meet regularly with people to talk life, and often they're searching for answers about what to do regarding finances, relationships, addictions, frustrating individuals... I attempt to avoid informing anyone how to live his or her life- I'm not smart enough, even if I thought that was my job. Instead, I like to help cultivate intimacy with God aimed at obedience to him, rather than create a dependence on me. So, assuming they root their identity in the vine- or at least are in the process of moving in that direction- and assuming they have spent intimate time with him, I like to ask questions that help people see their situations more objectively. We tend to struggle in knowing how to respond to our own lives because the details become overwhelming, but when we're able to objectively look at our circumstances, most of the time we know what obedience looks like.

One question is the classic: "What would Jesus do?" Even more so, though: "What would Jesus do if he were you?" After seeking advice from a friend or pastor, followers of Jesus may be instructed to read their Bible for answers. But Jesus never struggled with Internet porn, credit card debt, road rage, or a social media addiction, making it difficult to know the right thing to do in any given situation simply based on the instruction of the Word. If however, Christians can become familiar with the character of Jesus expressed in the Word, attempting to imitate how he would respond in their shoes becomes more realistic. So become familiar with the person of Jesus in the gospels, how he treats people, how he approaches situations, recurring language

7 John 8:11

he uses… and then ask yourself what you think he might do if he were in your shoes.

Another question often inspires a "Eureka!" moment. I think most people know what needs to be done in any given situation; they just don't know that they know. Hence, I like presenting this question: "If you had a good friend going through exactly what you are going through, and she told you all her feelings, thoughts, and interactions with God and people, and has come to the same place and conclusions you are at right now, what advice would you give her?" Interestingly enough, most of the time they give themselves great advice.

The goal here is to help another view himself almost as if he were watching a movie or TV series about his own life. When we're wrapped up in a good movie or TV series, the creators have figured out how to inspire our thoughts and emotions to want characters in the story to make specific decisions. For example, have you ever found yourself talking at the TV because of the way a character was making decisions? If we put ourselves on that "screen" regularly, we would be talking at the screen regularly too. If you can figure out how to zoom out from your life for a few moments, I bet you can give yourself great advice.

To add to this, my friend Nathan Kollar once used this illustration: imagine God hands you a blank page contract and asks for your signature at the bottom. The catch is that he gets to write the contract whenever he wants, however he wants, and change it whenever he wants. Can you sign it before you know what will be on it? This is discipleship. And God's hope is that we could respond: "Whatever you want to do with me, in whatever time, and for whatever purpose, my answer is yes." That is obedience.

Lastly for obedience, I thought it appropriate to add some thoughts about an element of obedience to God I've heard from only a few teachers. I have known a number of people who appear to be neurotic or obsessed with obedience to God. For some, it's to the point where they live most moments in fear of missing God's will for their life, of being disobedient on accident, even after they have ardently sought God's voice. I don't think this is what Jesus had in mind when he talked about abiding.

Many of us have been there. We have a significant decision to make. We prayed about it; maybe even fasted. We sought wise counsel from Scripture and from those in spiritual leadership over us, and still have no idea what to do.

I believe the ultimate illustration of our relationship with God is that we are his children. We are beloved sons and daughters of an affectionate Father. Moreover, I have encountered him to be a Father who is developing and growing us to become persons who can make decisions on his behalf. For example, as I write this, I have a two-year old daughter named Aria. Currently I have to give her instruction regarding all of her life. I teach her to say please and thank you, to frequently eat vegetables, and to faithfully support the Raiders- sorry, I had to throw that in. There will come a day, however, when my informing her of how to live must turn to reminders, and then eventually from reminders to simply being there for her. When Aria becomes an adult, I hope she will still come to me for advice about confusing or difficult situations, but she won't need to ask me anymore about manners, about nutrition, or about supporting the Raiders- although she may need encouragement on this one during trying seasons...

Similarly, our relationship with our heavenly Father progresses in much the same way. When we are new believers, he has to inform us regularly of how to live. We need to be taught that real love is choosing to love those who fail to reciprocate, that we should not indulge in sin because it destroys life and wholeness, and that his grace is bigger than we think it is. Yet, as we learn to be intimate with our Father, we catch his heart; his voice gets in us. We begin to understand what he loves, what he wants for us, what he desires from us. And there comes a day when we will be unsure about his will in a situation, so we pray, fast, seek wise counsel, then receive from God this response: "I trust you. I know your heart. I know you want to please me. Do what you like here; just put me in the center of it." Or to paraphrase St. Augustine, love God and do what you please.

The abiding life brings us beyond the point of needing signs to understand God's direction for our lives. When Christ's abiding presence becomes our day-to-day guide, his direction begins to morph into a sort of unconscious response; a gentle nudging of the Spirit in us. Much like ice skaters gliding on the ice together, we begin to know the upcoming movements of our partner without the need for words.

Please hear me: this is not permission to simply live however we want, whenever we want. This should come after questions like, "What would Jesus do if he were me?" and "What would I recommend to a friend?" It comes after seeking God for direction, after fasting, after pursuing wise counsel. After all that, if you still don't sense a pull in a direction by the Spirit of God, I simply suggest that maybe God is trusting you to make a decision on his behalf because he knows you want to please him and will place him at the center of the decision. He is in fact training us to be children he can trust with decision making.

Once again, to sum up the three-fold nature of abiding for me, it comes down to rooting our identity in the vine, choosing a lifestyle of intimacy with him, and then being obedient to what he asks of us. If we make the decision to faithfully walk down this trail, the grace of Christ will fill in the cracks where we fall short.

And this part is so important: *more than wanting us to always "get it right," God wants surrendered hearts. What pleases him most is our desire to please him.*

What I love about using this three-fold grid for abiding is that each element feeds into the others. When you root identity solely in your branch-ness in Jesus, your desire to be intimate with him increases, which increases your desire to be obedient to him, causing you to return in rooting identity in him at a deeper level.

I also want to acknowledge that this process demands humility- knowing we cannot even abide well without the help of the one in whom we will abide. We need the active grace of Jesus Christ even more than we think we do. I have found this to be a wonderful place to begin with abiding.

Presence in the Moment

Have you ever heard the phrase, "Be present in the moment"? While sounding existential or Confucian, it might stir up some thoughts for you: "How can I not be present in the moment? I'm here right now. How can I be present in another moment? I don't ever recall being present in the past or future, although I'd love to experience that..."

For me, it took years to understand presence in the moment, and I bet I've only scraped the surface of its complexity. What I've come to understand, though, is abiding is near impossible without it. We see Jesus touch on this principle in the Sermon on the Mount: "Therefore do not worry about tomorrow, for tomorrow will worry about itself. Each day has enough trouble of its own." Essentially, he's making the argument that you can, to your own detriment, exist in the present while living in the future or the past.

My favorite author, Brennan Manning, tells a wonderful story about presence in the moment:

> "A monk was being pursued by a ferocious tiger. He ran as fast as he could until he reached the edge of a cliff. He noticed a rope hanging over the cliff, grabbed it and shimmied down the side of the cliff... the monk glanced down

and saw a big, jagged rock five hundred feet below. Then the monk glanced up and saw the tiger poised over the cliff. Just then, two mice began to chew on the rope. What to do? The monk looked down at the face of the cliff, saw a strawberry growing, reached out, plucked it, ate it and cried, 'Yum-yum. That's the best strawberry I've ever tasted.' "[8]

The point: if the monk had been preoccupied with the rock below- his looming future- or with the tiger above- his gnarling past- he would have missed the strawberry God was offering him in the present moment. Precisely, presence in the moment.

This component is central to the abiding life. Sure, you can root your identity in Christ, be intimate with him, and even be obedient to what he is asking of you, *but the profound truth of abiding is that you cannot abide in the past, nor can you abide in the future; you only have the ability to abide in the present moment- here and now.* As we attempt to live in the past or future, we end up engaging in a form of sleepwalking; here but not fully here, only partially alive to what is happening around us.

I believe the most important thing you can know at any given time is what God is doing in your life at this present moment. I remember encountering a deep sense of sorrow one day after pondering over this: When I was in 5th grade, I couldn't wait to get to 6th so I could be in the youth ministry at my church. When I hit 6th grade, I couldn't wait to get to junior high so I would be out of elementary school. When I hit junior high, I couldn't wait for high school. In high school, I couldn't wait to graduate so I could get out of my parents' house and move on to university life. In college, I was in a hurry to graduate and become a pastor. And then as a pastor, I remember sitting at my desk as I read the story of the monk and the tiger; soon after thinking: "I wonder how

8 Brennan Manning, *Ruthless Trust: The Ragamuffin's Path to God*, 140.

many strawberries I missed in previous present moments that I will never get back. I wonder how many situations or seasons I had to come back to because I was not aware of what God was doing in the previous 'now' moments." Unfortunately, the popular phrase, "I can't wait..." often leads us to miss what God is working on in the moment.

Not long ago, I spent a morning with God at a large and beautiful cemetery in LA. I find that sitting amongst the dead causes one to reflect differently than when he or she is with the living. That morning I sat under a large tree, overlooking the well-manicured, rolling hills. The moment invited me to meditate on the nature of time. It moves. Always forward; indifferent to emotion, memory, individual, and circumstance. I find it wonder-some that that experience of time is subjective. In one moment, time seems to crawl; in another, it moves swiftly. Most often, though, when we look back, time seems to fly.

I think back to when I graduated college. As I sit and write today, my college graduation was almost ten years ago, but it feels like maybe three or four years. I think back to when my daughter was born. It was a little over two years ago, but it feels like three or four months. To be transparent with you, one of my greatest fears is waking up twenty, thirty, forty years from now asking where my life went. I fear that challenging seasons will cause me to simply want to survive, to merely make it to the end of the day or the end of the season, missing the beauty of what God is intending me to experience- the strawberries.

Sitting amongst tombstones that day, I wondered how fast time seemed to move for the dead man who lay beneath me. From learning to ride a bike as a child, to finding love, to celebrating the birth of his grandchildren, to laying on his deathbed. How fast did that seem for him? And why should I expect it be any different for me?

The vital point not to be missed is that *the true prayer of an abider is one attentive to what God is doing in him or her right now.* Now, God may or may not inform us precisely of his work, but abiding turns our hearts to him via a deep longing in how we can participate with his already present work in our lives.

And for our future thinkers, our visionaries, I want to note that abiding actively and presently remains in the vine, which at times will include planning for the future. God calls us in moments to look forward, to goal set, to strategize for where he wants to take us. Obedience to the vinedresser will at times also focus on bringing redemption or healing to our past. Sometimes we have to go backwards to move forward. Ultimately, though, obedience is being conscious and aware of what God is up to, what he is pruning, and what he is producing in us right now, with the awareness and trust that God touches both our past and future with *his* reach.

I now turn the mirror to you. Currently what strawberry in your life is being overlooked because you're too focused on your past or your future? Don't waste your present moment. Maybe this is a wonderful season. God is forming in you now what he wants to use later through you. Maybe you are in the most uncomfortable season of your life. God is also forming in you now what he wants to use later through you. Be intentional about not wasting it, or you might have to come back around to it again later.

Don't just survive. Don't just make it to the end of the day. Abide today. What is God up to in your life, right here, right now? Be receptive to that, because it is intended to inform and give life to every other aspect of your life.

I heard once that there is no past or future in God. There is only now. The past is merely a compilation of memories; the future exists only as expectancy and imagination for what is to come. I'm not sure there could be a better description for the environment of abiding. "Now" is the soil from which the vine grows. Abide in the vine and be present in this moment; there are many strawberries waiting for you.

Jesus, help us not to miss the moments we were created to enjoy.

"I am the true vine, and my Father is the vinedresser...
Abide in Me, and I in you.
As the branch cannot bear fruit of itself
unless it abides in the vine,
so neither can you unless you abide in Me."
JOHN 15:1, 4

Chapter 1
Questions For Personal Reflection and/or
Small Group Discussion

1. What other vines are fighting for your identity?

   ○ What the world says I should be. "IT girl" mentality

2. Is your identity currently rooted in God alone, is it shared, or is it not rooted in him at all?

   It's def shared. I think its initially rooted in him, but it wavers quite alot.

3. What does your regular, alone time with Jesus currently look like?

   Taking time with Him in nature.

4. What advice would you give to a friend who had your current life? Would you recommend he or she live the way you're living?

   yes! I love the way I live and love others! I would say to spend more time w/ God tho.

5. What strawberries might you be overlooking because you're too focused on your past or your future?

   - wedding prep
   - working at a great job
   - blessed w/ people + community

CHAPTER 2.1

FRUIT

-FINOYB-

> *"I am the vine, you are the branches;*
> *he who abides in Me and I in him,*
> *he bears much fruit,*
> *for apart from Me you can do nothing."*
> *~JOHN 15:5*

> *"We must understand that God is in charge*
> *of the outcome of our efforts,*
> *and that the outcome will be good."*[9]
> DALLAS WILLARD

What Is Fruit?

I have heard preachers exclaim that when we abide in the vine, we will bear unimaginable fruit. Congregations respond with a hopeful "amen," but then they walk out of the room clueless about what it means for fruit to actually result from their lives. How exactly does a follower of Jesus bear fruit? Observable fruit.

---

9 Dallas Willard, *The Great Omission: Reclaiming Jesus's Essential Teachings on Discipleship*, 34.

Practical fruit. And how can we make fruit bearing happen in our lives?

It seems, however, a backwards approach to talk about bountiful fruit bearing before we even agree on what fruit is. What was Jesus talking about when he mentioned fruit to his disciples? I assume this one has been debated over for centuries, and it seems to be a conversation we'll continue having until Jesus clears up the discussion in eternity.

In my research I've seen the fruit in John 15 described as many different things, but the definitions often seem quite surface level regarding Jesus's teaching on fruit bearing. To illustrate, let's say a student was asked to write an essay on the animal kingdom, but wrote a 15-page paper on penguins. Although penguins are an extraordinary part of the animal kingdom, they hardly sum up the entirety of the kingdom. A person could not make a valid argument that the animal kingdom *is* penguins. Similarly, if someone were to ask me, "Josh, in your opinion, is fruit defined by obedience to Christ, Christian converts, the love shared in the trinity, Christian character, the fruit of the Spirit found in Galatians 5:22-23, knowledge of God, our attitude, our behavior, our speech, union with God, or something else?" my answer would be, "Yes." I'm not sure Jesus was attempting to funnel down the definition of fruit to one seemingly "Christian" idea; I think he was up to something much grander.

I have wrestled with the idea of fruit for some time now, and here's where I eventually landed: fruit is simply the results and outcomes of our actions. Fruit is also the results and outcomes of the actions of God, Satan's kingdom, and other human beings. It is the future. It is the consequences of present moment decisions that will manifest in future present moments.

Earlier we saw that the first aspect of abiding is choosing a vine, which deals with the question, "In whom or what will we abide?" Because we have the power to abide in other vines, we also have the ability to bear the fruit of those vines. What I believe Jesus to be communicating is this: *we can abide in whatever vine we want, and as a result of our abiding, we will bear the fruit of that vine.* We *will* experience the result or consequence of abiding in that vine. Therefore, not choosing Jesus as our vine will result in our fruit being synthetic, artificial, and void of any real nutritional value. The only way to bear long-lasting, healthy fruit is to abide in the true vine.

For example, if we choose to abide in the love of material possessions, leveraging our influence and relationships to incessantly collect more, the fruit of our lives will be the result of our actions- possible credit card debt, an insatiable longing for more possessions, or broken relationships. If we choose to abide in the love of the game of sexual promiscuity, constantly searching for the next challenge and the hotter find, the fruit of our lives will be the result of our actions- loneliness, possible STD's, or accidental offspring. Likewise, if we choose to abide in the love of Christ, the fruit of our lives will be the result of our actions- Christlikeness, union with God, increased passion for the lost, or all of the above and then some.

Additionally, did you notice Jesus does not distinguish between good fruit and bad fruit? He just speaks of fruit. He told his followers if they would abide in him, they would bear fruit.

Which fruit would you say is healthy for you: strawberries or prunes? Both, right? But which one would you prefer to eat? Most would choose the strawberry. We must understand that Jesus's talk about abiding in the vine and bearing the fruit of that vine was purposed for glorifying the vinedresser- the Father. Although at times it may be enjoyable, fruit bearing is not about our enjoyment of the fruit. Fruit bearing is about Kingdom good over your good, which means sometimes the fruit of your life will be beneficial for the Kingdom of God while tasting terribly bitter.

The life of Paul is a wonderful example of this truth. His abiding in the vine and living in obedience to that vine led to what fruit? The results of his abiding: persecution, floggings, beatings, and ultimately getting murdered. Sure, it was for Kingdom good, but it had to be dreadfully unpleasant for Paul. Or look at Jesus's life. The fruit, the consequences of his actions: persecution, ridicule, arrest, and crucifixion. The fruit Jesus experienced as a result of obedience to his Abba was magnificent for the long-term good of the Kingdom of God, but it was terribly bitter to Jesus.

At the end of the day, we have to confront our expectation that following God is going to make our lives better. The center of God's will may be the most dangerous place in the world for you. Jesus never promised easier lives for his followers. In fact, Jesus said it would be difficult. Even more so, the abiding life may result in more discomfort than a life apart from Christ. Failure then should not be understood as experiencing bitter tasting fruit. Rather, *failure should be seen as distancing oneself from the true vine because of bitter tasting fruit.* While Jesus doesn't offer easy lives, what he does offer is his unceasing presence. And with his presence comes transformation for the heart of an abider, making joy an option even in pain.

FINOYB

If you noticed the title of this chapter, you might be wondering what FINOYB means. We'll get there soon enough. Until then, I'd like to set it up with what I find to be a valuable exercise.

As I explained previously, my understanding of what Jesus meant by fruit is results. Fruit is the consequences of our actions in the present moment. It is future; it is outcomes. Given this breakdown, I want to suggest taking a moment to work through categories of possible, future fruit in your life. Now, I understand that when an author asks us to stop reading, to take a moment and think about something, the efficient part of our minds wants to rush to "the point." But stay with me for a minute and allow this illustration to take effect.

Below is a list of areas in our lives where fruit has the potential to manifest. It is not meant to be exhaustive, but it will do for now. Take a moment to go through some of these areas and think about the possible fruit from these parts of your life- possible outcomes, results, and consequences from these categories.

For example, in the "finances" area, there are many possibilities of outcomes or results based off the actions of God, Satan's kingdom, yourself, and others. Someone could hand you a million dollar lottery ticket today. You could be a victim of identity theft and lose everything. You could sell all you have and give the money to the poor. You could invest in the stock market and win big, lose big, win small, lose small, or come out even. You could bless your church or another organization with a financial gift. You could save every dime, or spend all you have the moment you get it. As well as everything in between... and you would experiences the consequences of these decisions and outcomes. The fruit- possible results to decisions that can be made in the present moment.

In the area of "relationship with a significant other," you could never find one. You could find them tomorrow and get married. You could find them when you're 80 years old. You could die tomorrow before you find one. You could be married now and they could leave you for another. They could cheat on you but ask for forgiveness. They could love you better than you love yourself. They could bless you with many children. They could be unable to produce children. As well as everything in between... and you would experiences the consequences of these decisions and outcomes. The fruit- possible results to decisions that can be made in the present moment. I hope you get the idea.

The aim here is to think through as many possible outcomes of what could happen in each area of your life. I have found this to be most effective if you write it all down or type it out so you can see all the possibilities in front of you, but at least do it in your head. Take a moment now with some of the areas listed below, and maybe ones not listed as well, and work through possible outcomes in each area.

Finances	Relationship with a significant other
Health	Vehicle/Transportation
Job	Church involvement
Kids	What others think of you
Schooling	The city in which you live
Housing	Your emotional well being
Friends	Your spiritual formation

Hopefully, you have constructed a rather large collection of possible results and outcomes for your future. Now look at this huge mass as a whole, realizing the mass is actually much bigger than you are able to construct in your mind or on paper. I want to ask you now, whose job description does fruit production fall under: the vinedresser, the vine, or the branches? Another way of asking the same question is: which one of these three is responsible for creating a fruitful vine? The answer: the vinedresser alone. The vine simply does what the vinedresser desires, and the branches are only told to do one thing: abide in the vine.

Do you remember at the beginning of the book reading through John 15:1-11? Jesus clearly explains who fills these three roles in the story: the Father is the vinedresser, Jesus is the vine, and his followers are the branches. As you hopefully recall from the first chapter, we must begin with identity. Identity tells you who you are, whose you are, and therefore, what your job is. You, the reader, are nothing more than a branch. You belong to the vinedresser, and your job is nothing more than to abide. *This all means that fruit is none of your business.* Once more, and slowly, Fruit Is None Of Your Business. FINOYB. I repeat this because, in all honesty, this idea has changed my life.

Fruit is none of your business. Everything you were able to construct in that mass of possible outcomes for your future, including other possible outcomes you failed to think up, falls into the category of fruit, which falls into the category of the Father's work, which means it is none of your business.

For most, this notion seems counterintuitive, but this is truth: *abiding is not the natural result of fruit; fruit is the natural result of abiding.* So as we gain understanding and discipline in our ability to abide, our ability to bear Kingdom fruit expands naturally as well.

To expound a bit more, the line, "Fruit is none of your business" is a phrase spoken into me by my pastor, Bill. For years he has been a non-anxious presence in my life; someone not impressed by me one bit- we all need at least one person like this. When I was younger, I regularly laid out my stress and confusion before Bill. He never told me how to live. He simply asked questions, re-presenting my life to myself, listening myself into my own story. One day he told me fruit was none of my business. I thought I understood. I had no clue. I came back weeks later with more stress and anxiety about the possible future. He responded the same: "Fruit is none of your business, Josh." I replied, "Yeah, yeah, I know…" I didn't. Not yet.

He told me this for years, actually. Each time I thought I understood it a little more. Maybe so, but I remember the day it clicked at a deeper level. I came to him while in my first ministry position. I told him, "Bill, I spend hours in preparation for my sermons. I study in lexicons and commentaries. I spend time with the Spirit, asking what she wants me to speak on. I study hard; I prepare well and then get up to speak. And what are people doing during my sermons? Some talk. Some text. Some fall asleep. Few take notes, and I wonder if any of them remember anything I say. I'm not even sure they care about my preaching. But it's good preaching, Bill. I'm a decent speaker and I have good application. They don't get it." Once more he responded, "Josh, fruit is none of your business." But this time he probed into it more than he had in previous conversations- maybe he knew I lacked the range to understand it before.

He asked, "Last week, in your preparation and delivery, did you do what the Father asked you to do?" I nodded yes. For some reason, what he said next stuck: "Then you can lay your head to rest at night stress-free and worry-free because you did what the vinedresser asked of you. The fruit of your obedience is his. The fruit of your sermon- whether people laugh, talk, sleep through, understand well, or are completely transformed by it- is the Father's. Your only job is to do what the Father has asked of you. Fruit Is None Of Your Business."

The light bulb went on. I got it, and I'm still getting this: the results, the outcomes, the consequences of what I preached on were all fruit. As a branch, my only job was abiding well and then doing what the vinedresser asked of me. That next week, I remember praying, preparing, preaching, and then sleeping better than I had in weeks because I did what my Abba asked of me.

The phrase, "Fruit is none of your business" is something I grappled with for years. It was something Bill spoke to me and into me, gently and with patience. And through grace, eventually this truth became *my* truth. I still wrestle with its implications, but it no longer exists as something Bill used to tell me. It is now ground on which I stand before the cross of Jesus. As I have opened myself to being formed through this truth, grace has transformed my mind and changed the way I approach life.

And now I share it with you, not as a mindset to be grasped, but as a drawing force that affects every decision made. While FINOYB has changed me, learning to release fruit is one of the hardest things I've ever done. I invite you to join in being wonderfully wrecked by this transformation as well.

CHAPTER 2.2

FRUIT

-RELEASING FRUIT-

> *"I am the vine, you are the branches;*
> *he who abides in Me and I in him,*
> *he bears much fruit,*
> *for apart from Me you can do nothing."*
> ~JOHN 15:5

> *"We must understand that God is in charge*
> *of the outcome of our efforts,*
> *and that the outcome will be good."*[10]
> DALLAS WILLARD

Two Challenges

F ruit is none of your business. It's easier said than done, and the difficulty in changing paradigms here is two-fold: learning to identity fruit, and then learning to release it. And we have to figure out how to do both well.

---

10 Dallas Willard, *The Great Omission: Reclaiming Jesus's Essential Teachings on Discipleship*, 34.

To start, identifying fruit requires pinpointing where we are re-sults-minded. We can begin by asking questions like these: "Where in your life are you trying to produce an outcome? Where in your life are you focused, anxious, or worried about producing a specific result?" If you have the humility and objectivity to search for answers to these questions, you can know precisely where you're fruit-minded. And to say it again, fruit is none of your business. Your business is abiding.

For years I struggled in being able to identify the fruit of my life in order to release it to God. To take all of life and filter it through the lens of identifying fruit and then releasing fruit to the vinedresser is a significant challenge. I have, however, come across an effective tool in helping to identify fruit quickly. I call it "the Triangle."

While working on my master's degree, I was sifting through some of Cynthia Bourgeault's work on centering prayer. In it she unpacks an idea from her mentor, Thomas Keating, who wrote about what he calls the "three emotional programs for happiness."[11] Reading through it my first time, I wasn't much impressed. But when I came back to it a second and third time, I realized I was under the influence of a force I had never even heard of. I processed and regurgitated Keating's thoughts for some time, and eventually, because many of us are visual learners, I drew up a diagram to illustrate what Keating was describing.

---

11 Cynthia Bourgeault, *Centering Prayer and Inner Awakening*, 95, 137.

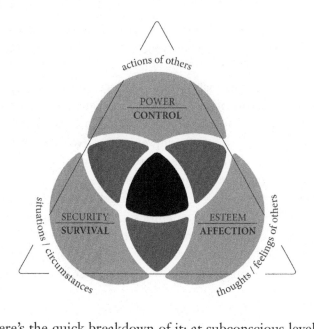

Here's the quick breakdown of it: at subconscious levels in all of us, we have three cravings fighting for our perceived happiness. These cravings attempt to convince us that if we can master these three areas of our lives, we will be happy.

The first area is what Keating called *Power/Control*. It argues that if you can simply make the people in your life do what you want them to, if the people in your life would just live, speak, and make decisions how you would like them to, you will be happy. If, on the other hand, people are not living how you would prefer them to, you will experience frustration, stress, anxiety, and fear.

Now, the stronger the grip of this craving on us, the more devastating it will be when we realize we cannot make others live how we'd like them to. Sooner or later, we will run up against a situation where we have no control, where people are not responding how we want them to, and it will feel like the end of our world.

We must learn to accept that we cannot control the people who make up the world around us- collectively or individually. The ones who have figured this out have stopped trying to exert power over others, and have learned to focus solely on controlling themselves. Self-control, in fact, decreases the drive to control those around us. This is probably one of the reasons why self-control is in the list of fruit of the Spirit in Galatians 5. In resisting this craving, we fight for contentment in the simple act of letting go of control over others, of influencing people to live the way we see fit, realizing we are actually not in control of anyone except ourselves-and sometimes, not even that...

The second area is what Keating called *Security/Survival*. It argues that if you can make situations and circumstances turn out how you want them to, if situations will just end up how you think they should, you will be happy. If, on the other hand, situations do not turn out in your favor, you will experience frustration, stress, anxiety, and fear.

This craving fights for safety and convenience. We subconsciously, and even consciously, attempt to make sure our world is not going to fall apart. "How much money I make matters, what I eat matters, where I work matters, what I drive matters, because they all play into my survival. I need to be happy, and I can't smile if I'm dead."

Therefore, we struggle to make sure the situations in our lives turn out the way we want them to, because we believe if they go as planned, it will make life enjoyable. But much like the issue of power over people, we have no control over situations either. What we think to be a controlled situation in our lives may better be described as chaos duct taped and super glued together.

Maybe you feel like you've gained some sense of control over how things turn out in your life. I did too- for a while. But eventually you will find yourself in the middle of a situation bigger than you, and you will be left helpless to the forces pushing against you. Unfortunately, whatever power you feel you have over *Security/ Survival* is only an illusion. Eventually we breathe in humility: "No matter how much I try, I cannot make situations and circumstances turn out how I want them to."

The third area Keating called *Esteem/Affection*. It asserts that if you can make people think and feel about you how you want them to, if people will just come to know and understand you how you would prefer, you will be happy. If, on the other hand, others do not perceive you as you would like them to, you will experience frustration, stress, anxiety, and fear.

With recent brain mapping, we're now able to see how the brain development of adolescents is different than in adults. When in the presence of peers, the reward circuitry in adolescents is more activated than in adult brains. Dopamine rushes into the prefrontal cortex to provide hormonal jolts that cause adolescents to act in ways that cater to the reactions of their peers. This is why teenagers and young twenties often make blatantly dumb decisions, and are particularly susceptible to social feedback, approval, and rejection. But how many adults do we all know that we'd argue have never developed beyond this type of brain activity?

Deep within us all is a potent longing for acceptance from those around us. If we think people like us, or at least if we think people respect or think highly of us, we wind up in happiness. If we think others don't care for us, we subconsciously either fight for that esteem, or feel worse about ourselves because we don't have it. We end up rationalizing that if the majority of people we know think well of us, especially the Christians, we're probably doing something right. Unfortunately, it's just not true.

To illustrate, I refer to what Charles Horton Cooley called "The Looking Glass Self," which birthed the phrase, "I am not what I think I am and I am not what you think I am. I am what I think you think I am." Go ahead; read it one more time- most people don't get it the first time.

Allow me to translate. Many people do not live based off what they think about themselves. Many people don't even live based off what others are thinking about them. Many people actually live based off what they think others are thinking about them, which most of the time is not even accurate. This type of life is lived, or at least attempted, inside the minds of others.

Those yet to discover who they are, who struggle with identity issues at the deepest levels, will set up camp in "I am what I think you think I am." If they think others will like them more or will think more highly of them because of a certain lifestyle, whatever it may be, they will continue in that lifestyle. Ultimately, they live their lives behind a mask- being, speaking, doing, feeling, and wanting based off what they think others are thinking about them.

When the craving for *Esteem/Affection* has a grip on us, we are driven by the desire for recognition and love. It will literally live through us, making decisions and producing actions based entirely on the superficial desire for like, respect, and love. Even further, it creates in us a subtle longing to present a perfected image of ourselves to those around us in attempts of being admired by all yet known by none.

Now when we zoom out, we see that these three little monsters have the tendency to form a sort of triple-helix strand around each other, affecting and influencing each other in ways unbeknownst to us. Here's a practical example: "I need a raise if I want to continue putting food on the table for my family. But I'm going to need to convince my boss to give me that raise. And I'm going to need to further impress him so he will give me the raise, so I can continue putting food on my table." Essentially, this situation claims: "I need to produce a certain outcome in my situation, but I'll need to make someone do something for me first, but I'll need to change the way that person thinks of me in order for him to do what I want him to, so my situation will turn out how I want it to."

To make matters worse, the problem is not merely that desires for power, security, and/or affection exist in us. It's that they often exist at such a depth that we end up rooting our identity in these cravings. They become the center from which we exist. Our lives are then defined by our ability to master power over others, control situations, and make people like or love us more. And when these desires have a white-knuckle grip on our souls, to the point where they define us and even decide actions for us, we wind up believing the better we master these areas of our lives, the happier our lives will be.

For many, success is nothing more than mastering the Triangle, and the most successful people in their minds are the ones who have mastered it well. The failure in this type of thinking, though, is that we will never gain complete control over these three areas in our lives. Any trace of mastery we currently have over them invites us into a constant state of anxiety in hopes of controlling the next season, because these areas of our lives are constantly trying to unwind themselves from our grasp. Eventually we realize the only way to have all our ducks in a row is if they're all dead.

The crux of this battle is found in the courage to admit to ourselves and to others that we are helpless. Brennan Manning notes, "The moment we acknowledge that we are powerless, we enter into the liberating sphere of the Risen One and we are freed from anxiety over the outcome."[12] While helplessness may come across weak to some, admitting we have no control over the Triangle is simply accepting the reality our situation: *the only thing I have control over is my effort and my attitude.*

I've also experienced myself, and witnessed from others, that once we hear about these cravings we may want to deny they exist in us. But if you took an honest look in the mirror, would you have the courage to admit how much these have hold of your soul? Think about your family members, your coworkers, your friends, your acquaintances… How much do you need others to do and say what you think they should in order for you to keep your calm? Think about your job, your finances, your health, your

---

12 Brennan Manning, *The Rabbi's Heartbeat*, 85.

possessions... How much do you need the situations in your life to be "working" for you to remain composed in life? Think of the individuals in your life that matter to you in one way or another. How much do you need to be liked or esteemed by them to keep a genuine smile on your face?

If your sense of calm, your composure, and your smiles are dependent on these three to any extent, the Triangle has gripped you. And the level to which your contentment is based off these three cravings reveals the level to which you are attempting to control an uncontrollable force. Even further, the level to which your contentment is based off these three cravings reveals the level to which your identity is rooted not in Christ, but in the Triangle.

You may be thinking: "Okay, so what does this Triangle of yours have anything to do with fruit?" The answer? *The Triangle reveals precisely every area of our lives where we are fruit-minded.* The Triangle is completely and utterly about controlling results. It is about manufacturing outcomes.

Here is what's so fascinating about this force: ironically, we attempt to avoid stress by way of the Triangle, but the Triangle just so happens to be the cause of the stress we're attempting to avoid. To say that again, the Triangle promises happiness but actually produces stress. So we attempt to avoid stress through the machine that produces stress. It is entirely counterproductive in nature. The Triangle attempts to convince you that you have the ability to produce lasting results, to engineer fruit, but it is exactly why we experience anxiety and a deficiency of lasting fruit.

Now, you might be thinking: "What about goal setting? What about vision casting? What about strategizing for things to come? Do we throw all this out with the chase after fruit?" Hear me. I'm not making the argument that God wants us to neglect planning and strategizing. I love how Khalil Gibran once put it: "Our anxiety doesn't come from thinking about the future, but from wanting to control it." The truth is, we cannot control outcomes and we're not responsible for them, but we are responsible for how we contribute to them. Often obedience will lead us to plan well for what is to come. The point to be made here, however, is that *the more our happiness is attached to outcomes, the less happy we will actually be. Even worse, the more our identity is attached to outcomes, the further we drift from the abiding life.*

Christians love to quote Jesus on "not worrying about tomorrow" while they worry about today. I don't think that's what he was getting at. In fact, the danger of the Triangle is that it seduces us to live in a constant state of anxiety and stress over outcomes, while fear materializes in our lives. The Triangle trains us to be and do from a foundation of fear. I have watched many friends live this way, making decisions because they are afraid of an outcome, or paralyzed by fear to the point where they cannot move forward with the decisions they want to make. Being motivated by fear is a dreadful way to live our lives. My experience is, those who live from fear regularly wind up in a death spiral of regret.

I also think to Psalm 23: "The Lord is my shepherd, I lack nothing." For me, this is one of the most important verses in all of Scripture. The Lord. God. The Being in charge of all this. He is my shepherd. And because the Lord is my shepherd, I lack nothing. Think about that for a moment. I lack nothing because the Lord is my shepherd. What a powerful truth.

But let's look at the opposite of this verse: the Lord is not my shepherd, and I actually lack quite a bit. This mindset perpetuates abiding in the heart of the Triangle rather than in the heart of our true vine. If I lack much, my life is constantly in need of me controlling an outcome. On the other hand, believing the Lord is our shepherd and that we lack nothing inspires faith to trust him with the results of our lives, including the Triangle. In fact, the more we live out Psalm 23:1 in our lives, the less we will struggle with the Triangle on a day-to-day basis.

Since I have discovered the Triangle, I have yet to find an area of stress, anxiety, fear, hurt, even sin that does not find its root in one, or a combination of the elements of the Triangle. This is why I actually disagree with C.S. Lewis's notion that pride is the root of all sin. I know you can argue from both sides, but I believe the root of all sin is the desire for control. When God made man in the garden, he formed dirt and breathed Spirit into it. Man is a combination of dust and spirit that is given a will. At the core of who we are is will; we are given the permission and power to choose what we please. The paradox of this life is that God gives humanity will and then asks for it back.

Pride, on the other hand, can be understood not merely as thinking too highly of self, but rather as thinking inaccurately of self. It is a warped or distorted inward view, meaning it can be thinking too highly *or* too poorly of self. Humility, then, is an accurate inward view.

Therefore, pride is a consequence of will because it is the will that chooses our self-perception- intentionally or not. We have been called beloved of God; honored sons and cherished daughters of a heavenly Father, but our will decides whether or not we will accept ourselves as that. It is the will that wants to choose its own identity. Sure, pride and will both have influence on each other, but at the end of the day it is will that decides how we choose to view ourselves. It is the desire to control even our own thoughts about ourselves that births sin.

Follow me now:

- Your will holds the power to attempt or surrender control in your life;
- The Triangle reveals the three fundamental areas of your life where you will attempt control;
- And every area you attempt to control is fruit.
- Oh yeah, and fruit is none of your business.

I hope this is clicking for you. So let's get practical now. Maybe you're having a hard time with the fact that people in your life are not responding to their lives how you would prefer them to. Maybe you are in the midst of a difficult situation and you're attempting to control the outcome of that situation. Maybe you're living a certain way to produce an intended effect on the way people think or feel about you. Once again, the control over how people in your life are living, the control over situations, and the control over what people think or feel about you is all fruit; and fruit is none of your business.

I love the Triangle because it unambiguously exposes where we're attempting to manufacture fruit in our lives. Glance back at the Triangle and think about the places in your life where you're experiencing frustration. We get frustrated with people, situations, or the way we think others view us, and it's all because we have our minds fixated on outcomes- on fruit. But you were not designed to attempt control over anything except yourself. Your only job as a branch is abiding in your vine and trusting in the vinedresser's ability to produce fruit through you; which by the way, is far superior to your ability to produce it through yourself. FINOYB.

To come back to it once more, the underlying issue here is identity. When your identity is not solely rooted in the true vine, it will be founded on your ability to exert power over others, to control the situations you're in, and make people like and think highly of you. This, in turn, disables you from the abiding life.

Living in a culture infatuated with self, the Triangle seems to be as prevalent as Starbucks. People think they find happiness in their ability to master the Triangle, yet in reality, they only master the art of unknowingly tumbling further into lost identity. The command Jesus gave his followers to take up their cross and die daily is one addressing this very issue.

Who is the center of your world? To this question you can only respond one of two ways: you or Jesus. There are no other options.

St. Augustine once claimed that there are only two basic loves in our lives: the love of God unto the forgetfulness of self, or the love of self unto the forgetfulness of God. One of these statements is truer than the other for you.

There is additionally an unfortunate problem we have to sit with: I don't think the Triangle will ever be weeded out or over-come- at least on this side of eternity. It is far more powerful than we are. If you disagree, try to completely rid yourself of these three compulsions this week. You will fail miserably. Therefore, we just have to get better at responding to it.

The abiding life diminishes the desire for power over others. We learn to rest in Christ's instruction: to use the power and influ-ence given us to elevate others rather than manipulate or dominate them.

The abiding life crumbles our impulse to control situations and circumstances. We're eventually convinced that the only thing we control is ourselves- and most of the time, we're not even great at that. God is sovereign; we lack nothing.

The abiding life thins out our craving to be defined by how others feel and think about us. We realize instead that our world exists only because of the love the Father, Son, and Spirit have for us. We are the beloved.

No matter how hard we try to be self-sufficient, God is still the one who meets our needs according to the riches of his glory in Christ Jesus. The vinedresser is absolute. He has charge over everything seen and unseen. We do not have to exert power over others, attempt to control situations, or people-please because we have been charged to live unto an audience of one: the vinedresser. And we do so through our identification as a branch in the vine.

Take a sincere look at the Triangle. Where in your life are you attempting to exert power over others to maintain what you think is a sense of peace in your life? Abiding suggests surrendering that longing for power to Jesus. Ask him for help and wisdom in knowing how to use your authority and influence to serve and lift others above yourself as he does.

Where in your life are you wading in worry as you scramble to keep all your plates spinning? Abiding suggests accepting that your simple task is to be obedient to what your heavenly Father has asked of you. This provides you freedom to give your best and then trust that you lack nothing.

Where in your life are you compromising your convictions in attempts to influence the affections of others towards you? Abiding suggests allowing the love of Jesus, the only true vine, to be enough for you; to define who you are. The extent to which you stress over what others think of you reveals the extent to which you believe in the love of Jesus for you. Stop searching for love anywhere but in the arms of grace. His love for you and what he says about you is enough.

To sum up, once we have learned how to identify where we are fruit minded, releasing fruit is a task only possible with grace. It will be the challenge of a lifetime, but I encourage you today to choose your vine, accept your branch-ness, and trust that the vine-dresser knows what he's doing. Because he's really good at his job.

CHAPTER 2.3

FRUIT

-LIVING IT OUT-

> *"I am the vine, you are the branches;*
> *he who abides in Me and I in him,*
> *he bears much fruit,*
> *for apart from Me you can do nothing."*
> ~JOHN 15:5

> *"We must understand that God is in charge*
> *of the outcome of our efforts,*
> *and that the outcome will be good."*[13]
> DALLAS WILLARD

Begin with You and Jesus

At this point in the conversation, even though it is a one-sided conversation, I believe it appropriate to bring up that if you are serious about releasing fruit to the Father, it will require putting "you and Jesus" first, before moving onto the "you and others" part of Christianity. Essentially, Jesus's point

---

13 Dallas Willard, *The Great Omission: Reclaiming Jesus's Essential Teachings on Discipleship*, 34.

in abiding is that your mission each day is to tune your ears to the Father's voice and do what he says. What other people think, what other people do, however situations play out, is none of your business. The fruit of your life will be dependent on how well you have learned to focus your attention on you and Jesus alone. In doing so, you will be intimate with the Father, which leads to him telling you what he wants of you, which consistently leads to serving and loving others.

The irony is that "you and Jesus" Christianity results in caring for others better than when you begin with serving others and moving on to the "you and Jesus" part later. Many Christians appear to care for others well. They serve, they constantly offer to do more, and they're extremely faithful. What we can miss, however, is that man has an uncanny ability to serve others and offer sincere care from dysfunction and insecurity. Someone with extremely low self-esteem may enjoy acts of service because others wanting, and maybe even needing his services can act as a fix for his next high of getting a compliment. The workaholic relishes serving more because she lacks the patience to be still and enjoy silence and solitude. The most narcissistic of them all can pour himself out for others with a smile on his face because he knows his actions may lead to others thinking well of him, maybe even bragging about his good deeds to crowds of potential complimenters.

In contrast, "You and Jesus" Christianity is held together as a result of who he is and who you are. Your only job is to abide in him- find your identity in him, be intimate with him, and be obedient to him. When you do these well, it *will* lead to loving and serving those around you. When you abide in the true vine, you catch his heart and his passions, and consequently, cannot help but pour yourself out for others because your vine has transformed you.

Moreover, if our service to others is not founded on obedience to the Father, we can end up serving in places and ways the Father would prefer us to avoid, even if it seems beneficial. I think back to an illustration I once heard about freediving. Freediving is a form of underwater diving that relies on a diver's ability to hold his or her breath until returning to the surface, rather than relying on an external breathing source. Because divers know how long they can hold their breath, they set an alarm on their watches before each dive to inform them when to head back to the surface. Sadly, the number one killer of freedivers is "shallow water blackout." Divers descend into the deep, the alarm goes off, but something catches their eye, requesting their attention for only a few more seconds-maybe a fish they've never seen or an obscure coral formation. As they head back to the surface after taking only a few more seconds in the deep, they pass out only feet below the surface. Death by one more thing.

If we pay close attention to the life and ministry of Jesus in the gospels, we come to realize he disappoints a lot of people. Just because Jesus had the power to do something, did not mean he was compelled to. There were plenty of sick people he could have healed, but didn't. There were plenty of dead people he could have raised to life, but didn't. Why? *Because Jesus was more interested in obedience to the Father than giving people what they wanted.*

Similarly, if we want to impact people as Jesus did, we need to learn to disappoint people like Jesus did. Just because we have the power to do something does not mean we should. Learning to say "no" may in fact, save our lives.

Paul had something very specific to say about this as well. In Galatians 1:10 he writes, "For am I now seeking the favor of men, or of God? Or am I striving to please men? If I were still trying to please men, I would not be a bond-servant of Christ."

As a follower of Christ, there will always be one more situation needing your attention. One more person who needs your help, who cannot finish the day without your input, who will wreck his or her life if you fail to give immediate aid. The ones who serve out of insecurity are more likely to burn out because they are the ones forgetting to breathe. They forget to care for themselves first. Much like in a plane going down, your oxygen mask must go on first before you help others. You are no good to anyone if you're not breathing.

Interestingly enough, the word for the Spirit of God in the Old Testament is *Ruach*- translated breath or wind of God. He is literally the very breath in our lungs enabling our continued service. When we attempt to care for others before we let God care for us, burnout is on its way because we end up doing things the Father is not asking of us.

With fruit on our minds, we are easily seduced into "making stuff happen" for Jesus, while abiding is the only action he asks of us. In abiding well, we are informed of when to rest and when to care. If you begin with service, you may end up burning out fast; but if you begin with you and Jesus, you end up with a service that comes from the heart of God, along with his perfect timing. It's better for all of us.

Living It Out

Abiding explicitly means fruit is none of your business. This truth changed the way I perceive reality and relationships, and it is now my worldview. Jesus said, "My Father is the vinedresser, I am the vine, and you are the branches. Your responsibility is abiding well." I love this because it simplifies following Jesus. We need not worry about how things are going to turn out. We are challenged to simply focus our attention and intention on rooting our identity in Jesus, being intimate with him, and then doing what the Father asks of us. The rest is his. It actually is that simple.

You may be thinking by now, "That's easy for you to say in theory, but what does this practically look like? How is this exemplified in real life? Or even better, do *you* even practice what you preach?" While I wouldn't consider myself an exemplar of the faith, I have encountered quite a few situations where it appeared the Lord was testing how much I believed fruit is none of my business. Here's an example of a time my faith was tested and God's faithfulness shined through.

Clarity

Back in my mid 20's, I was pastoring at a church in Hawthorne, California. I loved my job and the people I served, but my direction would soon be changed because of a phone call. A church planter named Nathan Kollar called me up one day with a simple request. He, along with his wife and some friends, moved across the country and planted a church in Santa Monica called Clarity. They were gathering on Sunday nights and needed a drummer to fill in every so often. I was free most Sunday evenings, so I began drumming for them and quickly fell in love with the community's heart for God, each other, and their community.

Little by little I built a close friendship with Nathan, and over the next year and a half, he would end up asking me three times to leave my church and come be an associate pastor for him at Clarity. It sounded great, except for the fact that there was little to no money to pay me because the church was so young. I laughed the first two times. By the third time, I realized he was serious. He wanted me to leave my church, raise monthly support, and live each month on faith until the church could afford to pay me. Each time I told him I would pray about it, and I did, but if I'm honest, I admit I was waiting for the day the church would have enough money to pay me full time.

Fast-forward a little. It was April 2012, and I was attending the Southern California Network Conference for the Assemblies of God- our denomination's yearly pastor and staff gathering. I accompanied the staff from my church in Hawthorne. Nathan was there with his staff as well. The first night, I sat listening to a message from a fellow pastor about having the courage to go when it would be easier to stay. I felt the weight of the Spirit on my heart during this message; I knew what God wanted me to do. I went down to the altar that night, got on my knees, and told God I would go to Clarity when he told me the time was right. I talked with Nathan that night and told him what happened. I let him know I would leave my church when I sensed the "Go" from the Lord. Little did I know how soon that would be...

The next day we were sitting in a session with Rick Warren. I was taking notes, listening intently. Then Rick's voice began to sound like Charlie Brown's teacher. I strained to listen but only heard the words, "June 1st." I thought to myself, "Ha! Yeah right! This must be my subconscious thinking I'm super-Christian Josh that can raise monthly support in under two months." Again the voice: "June 1st." I told God in that moment, "Lord, if this is you, I need you to make it *real* clear. And I'm not talking about Rick's teaching vaguely touching on a similar idea that has to do with my situation so I can read into it. I need some crazy confirmation right now- like an angel from heaven. Seriously, God."

The reason I asked for such a blatant confirmation was because at the time, my brother was living with me. He was in law school and had no time for a job, so I was paying most of the bills for the both of us. If I messed this one up, it could mean both of us having to find a couch to crash on. Not to mention, I didn't want to tell the people at my church that I was leaving to go to another church if that was not exactly what God was up to.

My mind was spinning, so I began texting my mom: "Mom, I think God wants me to start serving at Clarity June 1st." I wrote it out and then stared at the text. I was afraid to push send. "What if I send this and I'm not supposed to go, but my mom thinks I should go in June and tells me I should, and then I act on that and screw it up for myself, my brother, and my church?!" Or the opposite: "What if she thinks I'm not supposed to go, but I really am?!" I stared at the text for probably ten seconds and then I heard a whisper. Nathan was sitting a few seats away from me and whispered my name. I looked over at him. In his hand was a note that simply said "June." I asked him in disbelief, "What the heck does that mean?!" He whispered back, "I'm just feeling June for some reason. I think you're supposed to come over in June." My mouth dropped. My stomach sank. My face went white. I asked God to be extremely clear on this one and literally, in minutes, he confirmed what he put on my spirit.

I knew God wanted me to go in June, but my mind couldn't make sense of it. God was nudging me to quit my job before the money was there, and trust that he would bring it in after I left- in a month and a half. I prayed, "Lord, are you sure you want me to leave and then raise support? Not the other way around?" Practically, it made more sense to raise support while I still had a job, rather than putting in my two weeks notice and then asking for financial help; but I knew what God wanted. I sought wise counsel, and in fact, was told by some that I should go find a side job first before I started with Clarity, to help pay bills until the support came in. I told each one of them the same thing: "It's not what God said to do." And then my poor brother- pun intended. His response: "Josh, are you absolutely sure God wants you to do this?!" He was genuinely scared about what God put on my heart.

My next move can be described by what Nathan likes to call "borderline stupid obedience." I quit my job and contacted everyone I knew. I exhausted my network, told them the story, and then waited. It was a scary month for me. My mind wanted to work through the finances, but my heart told me to trust God. It was a battle inside. "What if all the money doesn't come in? Am I going to need another job like some people recommended? Should I look but not apply? And what if people say they will support me but don't? Or what if they support me for a month and then realize they can't anymore?"

My mind was playing tricks on me. I had to shut it up. I knew I had abided well, I knew what the Lord wanted me to do, and I knew my only job now was obedience to the Father. The results of this decision were his business, not mine. The fruit of this decision was his business, not mine. I knew whether or not the money came in, my focus needed to be on obedience.

Marvelously, over the next two months I watched God take care of the fruit. Phone calls and emails poured in. I had people contact me that I didn't even talk with about the move. In eight weeks God raised enough monthly support to take care of my needs. I served at Clarity on monthly support for over two years, and each month I paid my rent, food was on my table, bills were covered, and I even had extra money to bless others with- which I made/make a priority every month.

As I sit and write this, I am now the lead pastor at the church. God is so faithful.

The point: abiding is our job; fruit is God's. Just do your part.

Abiding is Active

I also want to include here that abiding is never mere laziness. Abiding is not an idealistic living in the clouds that doesn't tangibly fit into real life. My message here is not to sit on your blessed assurance while God lives your life for you. Abiding is active; it causes movement. And it asks that we do our part while trusting God to do his.

To expound more, there's a fascinating relationship between our *being* and our *doing* in following Jesus. Living in this tension requires understanding our roles: God is responsible for transforming us, while we are responsible for living in line with his transforming work. What interrupts this beautiful interaction between being and doing is when we mix up our roles in this process. When we try to take care of both elements, attempting to live holy lives while transforming ourselves, we surrender to pharisaism. When we expect God to take care of both elements, assuming he will perform the work he has called us to while at the same time transforming our hearts, we surrender to laziness. The healthy tension between these two points is yielding our hearts unto God to transform as we live obedient and holy lives before him, which sets us up to be further transformed, which sets us up for more obedient and holy lives. We do our part. God does his.

The reality is, the Kingdom of God could work without us, but for some reason God desires our participation. *Abiding, then, does not labor out of necessity, but solely from obedience.* Identity in God, intimacy with him, and obedience to him informs us on how we are to participate with grace, *while not being responsible for the results of that abiding.*

I understand some of you are undoubtedly in situations close to breaking you. Maybe a loved one is slowly dying of cancer. Maybe you're doing everything in your power to find a job to pay the bills and put food on the table for your kids but nothing is coming through. Maybe your wife is separated from you and you're waiting for her to come home as she finds herself. *For too long we have been trained in fruit production rather than disciplined abiding.* We have been convinced we have the power to make people do what we want them to, whether they be our kids, our best friends, our spouses, or those who work for us. We have been influenced to think we can take a difficult situation and produce an outcome of our liking. We have been manipulated into believing we can control what others think and feel about us, while in reality, what we label control is merely an illusion.

I noted earlier how I believe the most important thing you can know at any given moment is what God is up to in your life. I also believe the enemy is threatened by your cooperating with God's work in you. This may sound obvious, but it should be stated anyway: *we are better off keeping our eyes fixed on Christ and acknowledging our enemy, than keeping our eyes fixed on the enemy and acknowledging Christ.* Therefore, one of Satan's subtle deceptions is to distract and then fixate our attention on himself, or how a situation might turn out, rather than on God's work in us through the situation. If he can fix our minds on fear of the results, convincing us of our ability to control a situation, we certainly will not be focused on the work of the Father in and through us.

This is likely why Jesus commanded his followers to seek first the Kingdom of God and his righteousness, and all the other things would be added to their lives. Seek first to allow the authority of God to function in your life. Don't seek fruit. Seek first obedience to him. Seek first to make him King in and through every decision you make, and the fruit will be added to you.

Moreover, while obedience to Christ sounds pleasant in theory, I will not downplay the difficulty of an obedient life. Nor will I downplay the difficulty of even figuring out what obedience to Christ looks like in your life, specifically. There is something incredibly mysterious, even ambiguous, about a life lived in obedience to Jesus. This is why I recommend Christian living in the context of Christian community. The Church is more than a group of people who gather on a Sunday morning for a church service. The Church is life lived together; Church as family.

Being attached to the vine means you are also attached to other branches. Therefore, just as the Christian life demands a commitment to Christ, it also demands a commitment to the community of Christ. Not to mention, we need each other more than we think we need each other. At the very least, Christianity calls us to a small group purposed around growing in Christ together, but in most cases, we would all benefit existing as part of a local congregation of believers.

Furthermore, life devoted to obedience to Christ is often challenging and confusing, but a heart set on obedience is the appropriate starting point. It sets us up for God to fill in the cracks where we fail and/or miss obedience to him. The encouragement of the world is to persevere until you get what you want- quite often, merely what's most comfortable for us. The encouragement given by Jesus, on the other hand, is to abide well, do what the Father has asked of you, and then trust that this is going to turn out good. And even if the outcome is not "good" in your perspective, you don't have to worry about it because you're not in charge anyway. The sooner you admit to yourself and to God that you are in control of nothing but the way you respond to God, situations, and the people around you, the greater your chance of bearing Kingdom fruit.

Ask for Heart Change

In order to be less fruit minded, we need a change of heart. But the only being with the power to cause deep heart change is God, so we need to ask him to do this work in us. One of the great examples of this type of ask is the Serenity Prayer. Many have heard of this prayer, maybe even prayed it before, but I wonder how many have prayed the whole prayer.

Originally it was an untitled prayer authored by the American theologian Reinhold Niebuhr. The full version goes like this:

> "God, grant me the serenity to accept the things I cannot change, the courage to change the things I can, and the wisdom to know the difference. Living one day at a time; enjoying one moment at a time; accepting hardships as the pathway to peace; taking, as He did, this sinful world as it is, not as I would have it; trusting that He will make all things right if I surrender to His will; that I may be reasonably happy in this life and supremely happy with Him Forever in the next. Amen."

What a beautiful request for a heart content with whatever fruit the vinedresser wants to produce. The central thesis of this book is that *fruit bearing is the Father's work.* This proves again and again to be ever challenging because most of us are products of control-cultures. We love to grasp at fruit, and we think we are quite good at it. However, the more we cling to in life, the less life we actually experience.

To finish off this chapter, I want to embolden you: you have been called to the wonder of abiding in the love of Christ; to marvel as a child before our God and Creator. Put you and Jesus first, and abide, abide, abide in him. Avoid seeking results. Pursue Christ with all your soul. And receive with confidence that whatever results from your identity in, intimacy with, and obedience to the vine, is the Father's business.

Fruit Is None Of Your Business.

> *"I am the vine, you are the branches;*
> *he who abides in Me and I in him,*
> *he bears much fruit,*
> *for apart from Me you can do nothing."*
> ~JOHN 15:5

Chapter 2
Questions For Personal Reflection and/or
Small Group Discussion

1. What future fruit- results, outcomes, consequences- presently concerns you the most?

2. How do you struggle with power/control (the desire to influence the actions of others)?

3. How do you struggle with security/survival (the desire to influence the outcome of situations)?

4. How do you struggle with esteem/affection (the desire to influence the thoughts, feelings, and opinions of others toward you)?

5. Which has been more of a priority in your life of late: fruit or abiding? Regardless of your answer, what steps can you take to move more in the direction of abiding, while releasing the fruit to the One in charge of it?

CHAPTER 3.1

PRUNING

-HOW PRUNING WORKS-

> "*Every branch in Me that does not bear fruit*
> *He takes away; and every branch that bears fruit,*
> *He prunes it so that it may bear more fruit.*"
> ~JOHN 15:2

> "*Would you know who is the greatest saint in the world?*
> *It is not he who prays the most or fasts most;*
> *it is not he who gives the most*
> *or is most eminent for temperance, chastity, or justice;*
> *but it is he who is always thankful to God,*
> *who wills everything that God wills,*
> *who receives everything as an instance of God's goodness*
> *and has a heart always ready to praise God for it.*"[14]
> WILLIAM LAW

---

14 Referenced by Dallas Willard in *Renovation of the Heart: Putting on the Character of Christ*, 141.

Optimistic Realism

One of the principal ambitions in following Jesus is abundant life. I agree with Dietrich Bonhoeffer that the cost of non-discipleship is greater than the cost of discipleship. Intimate union with Christ can lead to an increased wonder about life in God, peace beyond circumstances, and a love for God and others that radically transforms our world. Relationship with the triune God is the mystical and beautiful dance of a lifetime. As we shroud ourselves in the abiding life, we are sincerely and profoundly escorted into wholeness. However, I am continuing to realize that a life committed to abiding in Jesus is anything but comfortable.

I consider myself an optimistic realist. I am undeniably a "glass half full" type of guy, but I also like to know what's in the glass and what we plan on doing with the contents of the glass. Therefore, when it comes to the gospel message, I get suspicious of a fluffy, sugarcoated message with guarantees of blissful prosperity. The language we find in Scripture describing discipleship to Jesus is far from mere enjoyment. Baptism is symbolic of a chosen death to self; we are commanded to take up our cross daily and die; Paul loves the language of a bondservant- that's a fun one to jump into if you get some time… Just because we're offered the splendor of the resurrection does not mean we get to bypass sharing in the suffering of the cross. In fact, the way Paul communicates it is that he desired to know Christ through the power of his resurrection, and participate in his sufferings, becoming like him in his death.[15]

Moreover, I realize a chapter about pruning, in any book, has the potential to move swiftly into the conversation of evil and suffering in the world, but this chapter will purposefully avoid answering why bad things happen to good people. My emphasis here will center more on describing pruning and our response during pain rather than on suffering at large.

---

15 Philippians 3:10

Pruning

In John 15, Jesus claimed that branches not bearing fruit get thrown out, and branches bearing fruit get pruned so they can produce more fruit. The vine Jesus talks about in this illustration is the grape vine, and grape vines are pruned regularly for their own good. To prepare them for more fruit production, leaves, smaller branches, and even fruit get pruned in this process.

I've heard if a fruit bearing tree or vine is allowed to grow untouched, both the quality and the quantity of the fruit suffer. A wild grape vine will actually produce fewer grapes and fewer healthy grapes than a consistently pruned vine. This is because in an un-pruned vine, the nutrition designated for healthy fruit gets distributed to everything growing: extra branches, stems, and fruit that should not be on the branch any longer. An un-pruned vine will bear a large quantity of smaller, less healthy fruit, and the opposite is also true. *The purpose of cutting off unnecessary material, then, is to circulate the vine's life and nutrition to the vinedresser's chosen fruit.*

In my wandering through research on the care of fruit bearing plants and trees, I found another substantial reason behind pruning. Pruning is a necessity in fruit production because it ensures proper access to sunlight throughout the plant or tree. Have you ever noticed that often, the best fruit seems to be where the light is? One could argue pruning or cleaning a vine open to light is a chief consideration when working with grape vines. Creating access for light to move throughout the previously hidden places of the vine greatly increases the capacity of the branch to bear fruit. But again, practicality, right? What does this have anything to do with your life right now? Let's start with the "light" element.

Pruning for Light

Once more, you are simply a branch through which the vinedress-er wants to bear fruit, and one way he produces fruit in you is by bringing light to the parts of your life you want to keep hidden. Yes, your dirty secrets you would never want your grandmother knowing. The truth is, your skeletons only have power over you as long as they stay hidden in the closet. You want to strip them of their power? Bring them out and let them dance at the party. Now, I'm not encouraging you to plaster your deepest sins and ugliest secrets on a discussion forum online, but if you find yourself going out of the way to keep something in your life hidden, it's probably an issue that needs to be addressed sooner than later.

There are two elements at play here: one is keeping things hidden from God; the other is keeping things hidden from those we're called to journey with. Remember, for God to bear fruit in us, he will create access for light to come in and bounce around the shaded places of our souls that reek of sin, guilt, and shame. This involves both our personal walk with Christ as well as our communal walk with him.

Have you ever been in a church service, or maybe in some alone time with Jesus, and you sensed him point at something specific in your life? Possibly a destructive behavior you've loved and hated for years, heated jealousy over someone else's success, or even the way you treat rude acquaintances or apathetic waitresses? And then you hear that small, deep whisper: "I want that." The easy response in this scenario is, "How about a simpler issue, Jesus? I'm not ready for that yet." Or maybe we've learned to justify certain sin by how well we glorify God with the other parts of our lives: "At least I'm not still struggling with that old habit I dropped three years ago. And these other areas of my life are really thriving currently." Some of us are pros at this.

My telling God I know what needs to be pruned and what can be left alone lets both of us know what I think about our roles: that I think I can vine dress as well as he can. In doing so, I also inform the Father he is not as important as that thing I'm avoiding surrendering.

Another way to think of it: bring to the forefront of your mind the most important thing in your life; the thing for which you would sacrifice the most. Maybe a person, a job, a car, a dream, a hobby, or even a calling... Now let's say you were woken up in the middle of the night by Jesus. No doubt in your mind, this is Jesus, physically standing in your room. And he has a request: walk away from the most important thing in your life for the rest of your life. Oh yeah, and he will never tell you why, not even in eternity. If you cannot surrender it to Jesus in that moment, he is less important to you than whatever he asked you to lay down. And in line with the thoughts of Rabbi Abraham Joshua Heschel, I would argue that God is of no importance to you if he is not of supreme importance.

Like a stained glass window, in order for us to live out our created purpose and destiny, light must be allowed to ignite the fragmented pieces of our souls. Maybe you have some issues buried deep that you know the vinedresser has wanted to clean out, but you've kept it in the dark. Again, the only way those skeletons lose their power over us is by exposing them to light. We have to allow God to prune the shadowy parts of us if we hope to bear the good fruit he has in mind.

Secondly, there is a communal aspect to hiding. If you recall, hiding was a result of the fall, not of God's original creation. Fear, hiding, shame, and blame happened when Adam and Eve were convinced they knew better than God.

I've known a lot of Protestant friends who give our Catholic brothers and sisters a hard time about confession, but the Catholic tradition has a well-carved path regarding coming out of hiding. James was onto something when he urged believers to confess their sins to, and pray for, each other.[16] And if you look closely at the passage, we don't confess our sins to each other to be forgiven; that's what the cross was for. We confess our sins to each other to

---

16 James 5:16

be healed. In some mystical way, God has weaved the healing of our souls into the practice of intimacy with each other.

Dietrich Bonhoeffer communicated that the more isolated a person is, the more destructive sin will be in his life. He writes: "He who is alone with his sin is utterly alone... Sin wants to remain unknown... In the darkness of the unexpressed it poisons the whole being of a person."[17] We were not designed to do this whole "Church" thing alone.

There's a story about a conversation Dwight L. Moody had with a man as they stood around a fire in the cool of winter. The man was attempting to convince Moody that being involved in the Church no more equipped a person's faith to thrive than being apart from the Church. After the man was done ranting, Moody grabbed the tongs, picked up a hot coal from the fire and set it off by itself. They both watched as the coal burnt out. The man looked at Moody and said, "You made your point."

To further drill the idea, I'm reminded of one of Aesop's fables from the 6th century:

> "A lion used to prowl about a field in which Four Oxen used to dwell. Many a time he tried to attack them; but whenever he came near they turned their tails to one another, so that whichever way he approached them he was met by the horns of one of them. At last, however, they fell a-quarrelling among themselves, and each went off to pasture alone in a separate corner of the field. Then the lion attacked them one by one and soon made an end of all four."

For some reason, many of us have been convinced that "me and Jesus" can fix my life without the rest of you, but I have yet to

---

17 Dietrich Bonhoeffer, *Life Together: The Classic Exploration of Faith in Community*, 110, 112.

find support for individualistic Christianity in Scripture. I know this stands in opposition to the radical individualism of the western Church, but the Church of the New Testament, the *ekklesia* as expressed in Scripture, was never the building where people worshipped; it was always the *people* that worshipped together, no matter the building, or lack thereof. One person can no more claim to be the Church than a penguin can claim to be the animal kingdom, or a fingernail to be a body.

In choosing to hide the truth of our lives from other followers of Jesus, our honest beliefs are revealed: we think we have the ability to be a fruitful branch without other branches. Imagine a grape vine with only one branch on it. How ridiculous, right? Yet, no more ridiculous than a Christian attempting to walk out his or her faith without the intimacy and accountability of other believers. If we hope to succeed in following Jesus, we need each other more than we think we need each other. Or how the old African proverb puts it: "If you want to go fast, go alone. If you want to go far, go together."

God desires to bring light to darkness. He longs to bring to the surface those things we keep hidden from him and other believers. We rob ourselves of the lives we were built for because we are too stubborn, lazy, or proud. Pruning and cleaning are designed to bear healthy, nutritious, and flavorful fruit in us. Come out of hiding. Allow the vinedresser to bring light to the shadowy areas of your life, and then choose to let others walk with you.

Take a moment and do some soul searching. Is there anything you could not give to Jesus if he asked for it and offered you no explanation? Is there anything you hold as closely as your relationship with Jesus, even if it's a good thing? If so, I want to encourage you to lay it down. And to be clear, just because we lay these things at the feet of Jesus doesn't mean he will take them from our lives. But he does want priority. If you lack the strength or courage to surrender it, take the first step and ask Jesus for help in surrendering it. I believe there to be no greater prayer than simply, "Help me, Lord Jesus."

And then talk with someone you can trust. Maybe your pastor, a small group leader, or a close friend. Reveal where you struggle. Come out of hiding to someone you trust, and expose the dark places of your life to them so they can pray for you often and ask you how you're doing with it. We're less likely to run back to our sin when we know someone is going to ask about it later.

You cannot do this alone. For your own good, don't try.

Pruning Fruit

You may have experienced that as the Father prunes leaves and branches in us, it isn't necessarily a terrible process. Parts may be uncomfortable, but the process at large can be quite refreshing. For example, have you ever had a secret eating a hole in your chest until you let it out? Maybe you just told one person. Sometimes confession just feels good because the junk inside us was rotting. We end up realizing the worst part is often exposing the darkness to the light, because now the healing can happen.

Like expressed before, pruning is purposed for a balance between a sizeable amount of little, worthless fruit, and a small amount of portly, unhealthy fruit. This means that in the process of pruning, the vinedresser's desire for valuable fruit will lead him to prune more than just branches and leaves; he will also prune fruit off the vine.

Again, fruit can be understood as results and outcomes; it is the consequences of present moment actions of God, Satan's kingdom, others, and ourselves. What we are currently experiencing in life is the fruit of the previously present moment decisions of many. Fruit can be the people in our lives, our material possessions, job or school opportunities, the state of our health or finances, and even the current reality of our spiritual formation; which means fruit is not necessarily good or bad- it just *is*.

Additionally, I want to remind you that Christ told his followers that abiding yields fruit, and fruit glorifies the Father, but he says nothing about our enjoyment of the fruit. Many of us entertain this ridiculous notion that abiding in Christ makes wonderfully comfortable lives, but for many, obedience to Christ meant persecution, torture, and even martyrdom. Spilled blood became their fruit, but in the words of Tertullian, "The blood of the martyrs was the seed of the Church." So yes, it was great fruit, but not for them. For these men and women, the fruit of their obedience was extremely unpleasant.

So we come back to FINOYB. As a branch, fruit is none of your business. What fruit stays and what fruit gets pruned off is the vinedresser's responsibility. He, not we, decides what fruit gets to hang around longer. He, not we, gets rid of fruit that should not be on the branch any more. The decision to cut off fruit that is pilfering essential nutrients is the vinedresser's responsibility alone. Any extra material in us not contributing to the purpose for which he created us, he will remove, if we let him. So yes, that means pruning may be a painful experience for us.

It's said that a newly pruned grape vine is a sight to behold. Pruned, or cleaned grape vines appear to have been literally wrecked by the vinedresser. This process is not like mowing your front lawn or getting a dog's hair groomed; it more resembles a surgery. It can appear as though the vine has been irreparably damaged, and this appearance will hold throughout the season. But as severe as it may seem to the untrained eye, the vinedresser has enabled the branch with capacity to produce more fruit and healthier fruit than it previously could. Pruning has effectively made the branch stronger and healthier.

Have you ever felt that God snipped away something from your life? Maybe it was good fruit. Maybe it was even good fruit you enjoyed, and maybe while it was falling you tried to catch it with all your leaves, hanging onto it as long as possible. I get it; it's hard to accept being pruned. Pruning can hurt; it changes life as we know it. Allowing fruit to fall can be dreadful, but wanting fruit without pruning is like wanting health without exercise; it will not happen.

Pruning is a terrible trial, *but pruning prioritizes decided growth over comfort.* Larry Crabb describes it like this: every follower of Christ has two sets of competing desires- to love God and be loved by him, and for this life to go well. The battle is in prioritizing.[18] The question you need to ask yourself is, "Do you want what God has prepared for you, or do you want what you think you need?"

Once more we return to control. Who is your vine? Who is your vinedresser? If Jesus is your vine, the Father is your vine-dresser, which means he gets the control. All cleaning and pruning is his business, not ours. Our business is abiding. And as we decide to act in trust, we relax and stop trying to do God's job for him, because he's much better at it than we are.

---

18 Larry Crabb, *Soul Talk: The Language God Longs For Us To Speak*, 82.

CHAPTER 3.2

PRUNING

-OUR RESPONSE-

> *"Every branch in Me that does not bear fruit*
> *He takes away; and every branch that bears fruit,*
> *He prunes it so that it may bear more fruit."*
> ~JOHN 15:2

> *"Would you know who is the greatest saint in the world?*
> *It is not he who prays the most or fasts most;*
> *it is not he who gives the most*
> *or is most eminent for temperance, chastity, or justice;*
> *but it is he who is always thankful to God,*
> *who wills everything that God wills,*
> *who receives everything as an instance of God's goodness*
> *and has a heart always ready to praise God for it."[19]*
> WILLIAM LAW

---

19 Referenced by Dallas Willard in *Renovation of the Heart: Putting on the Character of Christ*, 141.

Responding to Pruning

The point here is not to explain why bad things happen. The fact is, bad things happen. Jesus said they would. We have an enemy who hates us, we live in a fallen world, we make mistakes, others make mistakes, and God even guides us into trials at times. Attempting to decipher which factor is at play, and likely a plethora of other dynamics at work as well, is something we should walk through with someone who understands well the reality of spiritual journeying. For your own good, find someone you can trust, who is gifted in walking with disciples, to journey with you through the muddy waters of your life. You were never intended to try to figure it out alone. All that being said, the point of this chapter is to bring attention to our response to pruning and difficult times.

I present two stories in Scripture of people's responses to hard times and unfavorable fruit. In Mark 4 we see the disciples in a boat with Jesus at night. A severe storm picks up- severe enough that many scholars argue it was likely even demon possessed. The experienced fishermen look back to the person who's supposed to be steering- the one on the helmsman's cushion- to find not only is Jesus not steering, he's using the cushion as a pillow for a nap. They proceed in yelling at him to wake up and then question his level of care for them, as they believe they are about to die.

We also have a story in Acts 16 where Paul and Silas are doing the work of God, ministering and casting out demons. They unfortunately upset a few too many people, and are thrown in the darkest, most dangerous prison. They're beaten, flogged, and left to rot. Their response, however, is to pray and sing hymns to God about their current situation.

The difference between these two stories is staggering and has considerable implications. When the disciples were faced with an extreme situation, even though Jesus was physically with them in the boat, their response was fear and anxiety. When Paul and Silas were faced with an extreme situation, even though Jesus was *not* physically present with them in prison, their response was trust and worship.

In Paul and Silas's situation, their freedom was dependent upon their worship. Freedom from the bitter tasting fruit of persecution was a direct consequence of their worship in the middle of it. And do you remember in the story whose chains fell off? Everyone's. Everyone in the jail was freed because of the decision of Paul and Silas to praise God in the midst of bitter tasting fruit, and ultimately, people were brought to salvation because of it.

This reminds me of a conversation in the film, Doctor Strange, where he's speaking with his mentor. She says: "Arrogance and fear still keep you from learning the simplest and most significant lesson of all." He asks: "Which is?" She replies: "It's not about you."

You may be in the midst of some terrible circumstances, but this "prison" might not actually be about you. *It may be that someone else's freedom is waiting for your worship.*

To funnel it down for you, one of our goals in following Christ should be allowing our fear and anxiety to be transformed into trust and worship. From, "I'm going to die" to, "I'm going to worship you." And your ability to do so will be dependent on who you believe Jesus to be, and how much you trust him.

Do you trust Jesus? It's easy to say we trust God, and the majority of Christians I know would claim they put their trust in him. Many can rapidly spew out the classics like, "Trust in the Lord with all your heart, and lean not on your own understanding..." but what about in the midst of a demon possessed storm? What if you are in prison for following Christ? Do you still trust him?

In his book *Good To Great,* Jim Collins writes a chapter on confronting the brutal facts of our situations, and he brings up what he calls the Stockdale Paradox, referring to Admiral Jim Stockdale, who was the highest-ranking U.S. military officer in the Hanoi Hilton prisoner-of-war camp during the height of the Vietnam

War. This man was tortured over twenty times during his eight-year imprisonment, lived out the war with no prisoner's rights, and had no set release date.

Collins tells of an afternoon he spent with Stockdale, in which he asked how Stockdale dealt with being a POW. Stockdale responded, "I never lost faith in the end of the story. I never doubted not only that I would get out, but also that I would prevail in the end and turn the experience into the defining event of my life, which, in retrospect, I would not trade."

Their conversation continued, and Collins finally asked, "Who didn't make it out?" His response: "The optimists." Why did the optimists not make it out? "Oh, they were the ones who said, 'We're going to be out by Christmas.' And Christmas would come, and Christmas would go. Then they'd say, 'We're going to be out by Easter.' And Easter would come, and Easter would go. And then Thanksgiving, and then it would be Christmas again. And they died of a broken heart." A long pause, then Stockdale said, "This is a very important lesson. You must never confuse faith that you will prevail in the end- which you can never afford to lose- with the discipline to confront the most brutal facts of your current reality, whatever they might be."

The Stockdale Paradox: *"Retain faith that you will prevail in the end, regardless of the difficulties. And at the same time, confront the most brutal facts of your current reality, whatever they might be."* Collins goes on to write, "What separates people, Stockdale taught me, is not the presence or absence of difficulty, but how they deal with the inevitable difficulties of life."[20]

Too often we attempt to run from the things God wants us to grow through. Brennan Manning once wrote, "If great trials are avoided, great deeds remain undone and the possibility of growth into greatness of soul is aborted."[21] *So if your circumstances are dif-*

20 Jim Collins, *Good To Great*, 83-86.
21 Brennan Manning, *Abba's Child: The Cry of the Heart for Intimate Belonging*, 105.

ficult and not changing, God is likely attempting to change you rather than your circumstances.

Throughout my life I've heard people say they trust Jesus because he would not put them through situations they can't handle. I could not *disagree* more. But it's Scripture, right? The verse is 1 Corinthians 10:13 and it says God will not allow you to be tempted beyond what you can bear. Jesus will regularly allow situations we can't handle to surround us, maybe even break us. Why? So we can learn to trust in his faithfulness over our own abilities.

Do you remember what God told Paul? That God's power is perfected in our weakness.[22] The breeding ground for miracles is an environment of brokenness and humility before God, which is exactly where he wants us.

Jesus told his followers to learn from him because he was gentle and humble in heart. These inspiring words may arouse a particular response from Christians today: "Lord Jesus, as you are gentle and humble in heart, so I want to be. Transform my heart to the likeness of yours." But what a dangerous prayer. Why? Because Jesus takes our prayers seriously- maybe more seriously than we do. As Manning notes, "We don't learn humility by reading about it in spiritual books or listening to its praises in sermons... Most often we learn humility through humiliations. What is humility? It is the stark realization and acceptance of the fact that I am totally dependent upon God's love and mercy, and it grows through a stripping away of all self-sufficiency."[23]

Sometimes pruning is simply about bringing us to the end of ourselves, because that is where we are most usable by God. And what I have experienced: the end of ourselves is where we find God.

---

22 2 Corinthians 12:9

23 Brennan Manning, *The Signature of Jesus: A Path to Living a Life of Holy Passion and Unreasonable Faith*, 135.

Many of us strive diligently to know God's will for our lives, but understanding his will is surprisingly simple. His will is that you would be transformed more into the likeness of Christ today than you were yesterday, and more tomorrow than you are today. This happens by pruning. The fruit you are carrying today, whether a result of God, Satan's kingdom, another person, yourself, or just this fallen world, may be exceptionally unpleasant. In fact, your circumstances may seem like they are about to break you. It may seem too heavy, too painful, too much... My suggestion for you: turn to worship. Even more so, thank the Lord for it. But how can we possibly thank God for painful situations? We begin by changing our prayer from, "I just want to know *why*, God" to "I just want to know *you*, God." This will set us up for the joy Jesus describes in John 15.

The Discipline of Thanksgiving

Here is where this all culminates: God's big plan for your life, his perfect will for your life, is Christ-likeness. He wants you to resemble him, and although God does not necessarily cause everything you experience in life, he at least allows it. I would never claim God caused all the things you've suffered. However, the reality is God could have prevented or redirected each negative thing from happening in the first place. Everything you have experienced in life has been permitted by God.

I also think grace is at work in our lives more than we realize. I thank God for the grace he's provided in ways of which I am completely unaware. I wonder how many times God stopped things from happening in my life I didn't even realize were about to- maybe a car accident he redirected, a health problem he healed before I knew about it, or even an emotional wound he prevented from taking root in me. Grace is bigger than we know.

Continuing in this line of thought, if everything I've experienced in life, good and bad, is at least allowed by God, it means he sees it fit to be part of my story, my redemption, my transformation to Christ-likeness. I experience only what he allows, only what he wills to be part of my shaping to the likeness of the Son. Another way of saying this: my entire life's experience to date has been calculated for my transformation to wholeness and the likeness of Christ. Therefore, my response to all of life, blessings and storms, seemingly bad fruit and good, should be, "Thank you," and "I worship you, God." My entire life's response should be a worship of gratitude.

I realize I have no clue what you've been through or how you are currently suffering, so I want to communicate empathy and compassion first. Terrible events occur every day in our world. And as tears of anguish fall before our God, I believe Jesus cries with the broken-hearted, even if he does allow difficulties. Scripture shows him to be a tender and affectionate God, suffering with the broken. But Scripture also calls us to a response in that brokenness. James writes that believers should consider it joy when they go through trials. Why? Because the testing of their faith produces endurance, and endurance, perfection: Christ-likeness. Or how its sister text claims in Romans 8:28: "God uses all things for good for those who love him…"

Ultimately, God's will is not a path we're called to walk; his will is how we decide to walk the path. God's will isn't the future episodes of our story; his will is how we choose to respond to the future episodes of our story. Although God may not have caused what you're going through, or have been through, he allowed it to occur and is using it for good. Therefore, our response should be thankfulness, *not despite what we're going through, but precisely because of it.*

Gratitude was not meant to be reserved for enjoyable moments. Gratitude should be the drumbeat that marks the rhythm of our lives. God wants to use all we go through to shape our likeness to his. Our perspective is too small, too insignificant, to claim anything could not or should not be used for our molding.

To put some action on this conversation, I want to walk through an uncomfortable episode from my own story. Now, I've noticed this discussion has the tendency to push us straight to grappling the extreme events of our lives, but sometimes it's wiser to begin with a less destructive event. So to try out the training wheels first, we'll start with something smaller scale. Later in the book we'll hit some heavier events.

I remember with great detail the week before finals week of my freshman year of college. I got into a serious car accident; it was not my fault, and my truck was totaled. That same week my computer crashed too (that was before I used a Mac). The combination of worry and stress became my reality. "God, how could you allow me to total my truck and allow my computer to crash right before finals!?" My response was fear and anxiety.

To make a long story short, I prayed over the blinking blue screen of my crashed computer and the entire hard drive was restored in front of my eyes. I was trying to sell my truck before the accident, and because of the accident the insurance company gave me more than it was worth, which enabled me to buy a car more trustworthy and better on gas mileage than my truck- which to a college student goes a long way. My back was also sore from the accident so I received back massages twice a week for six months on the other insurance company's dime. Oh yeah, and they gave me an additional two thousand dollars for the pain and suffering of the experience.

Half way joking, that week turned out to be quite a blessing. I can say that now. Oh the gift of hindsight… Or as Soren Kierkegaard noted, life must be lived forward, but it can only be understood backwards.

At the time I was particularly inconvenienced, furious at God, and anything but filled with joy. I see now the Lord was actually using that situation to bless me. My faith grew from watching my crashed computer return as if nothing had happened, and the car I was able to purchase because of the accident was a major step up from my previous vehicle. Whether or not God caused the accident seems like a non-issue to me now. How I responded to the situation and to God is far more important. I retorted, "How could you?" It should have been, "I worship you."

Please hear me; in no way am I trying to compare a difficult week of my life during college up against difficult weeks or months you have endured. Neither am I arguing that the week I previously described was the most difficult of my life; far from in fact. I guarantee some of you reading this book have gone through situations so painful you can barely even think about them, let alone describe them. The point of my illustration is simply to indicate how tiny my perspective was. Thankfully I was able to see months later how the Lord would use the situation for good, and even comfort, in my life. However, and this part is crucial: if I can only worship God when my circumstances are comfortable or enjoyable, I need to reevaluate my worship. *A heart of worship, a life of gratitude, has nothing to do with circumstances; it has everything to do with the posture of our hearts. True worship is conditionally independent.*

I cannot help but throw in here that the writer of Hebrews made sure to point out that Jesus, though he was the Son of God, learned obedience through suffering.[24] If the Christian life is fundamentally an imitation of Christ's life on earth, and he learned obedience through what he suffered, why would we learn obedience any differently?

To get a little more blunt, do you trust Jesus? Even if it appears that Jesus is sleeping when he should be steering your boat, and even if it appears that God is nowhere to be seen in the midst of terrible fruit, do you trust him? My pastor once told me, "The extent to which you stress out and are anxious about life shows the

---

24 Hebrews 5:8

extent to which you trust Jesus." Talk about a reality check. If we
don't trust Jesus, let's at least admit it. God wants us as we are, not
as we should be, because none of us are as we should be. Many of us
need to stop lying to ourselves, claiming to trust Jesus while we're
angry and stressed about the fruit of our lives.

I once heard about a missionary family on furlough, staying
at a friend's lake house. One day while the parents were preoccupied and their three children were playing out front by the lake,
the youngest child wandered down to the wooden dock and fell
into the murky water. As the oldest child screamed, dad came running out. Realizing what happened, he dove into the dirty water.
Multiple times he dove down grasping for his son but felt nothing. Taking another deep breath, he dove again and found his son
clinging to the wood beam holding up the dock. He pried his boy
off and brought him safely to shore. Confused, he asked his son
what he was doing under the water. His son replied, "Just waiting
for you, Dad. Just waiting for you." Trust.

Courage has been described not as a lack of fear, but in pressing
forward despite existing fear. It embraces peace in the face of difficulty. Trust likewise, should not be defined as keeping a distance
from fear or un-faith, but rather as a joyful confidence that relent-
lessly places faith in Christ whether or not our hearts or minds are
following suit. And I believe David is permission-giving on this
one. Many times in the Psalms, we read David expressing that he
put his trust in God. The funny thing is, if you trust someone, you
don't have to *put* your faith in him; you trust him. *Putting* is unnecessary if trust exists. Essentially David is saying, "God, I don't trust
you. Therefore, I'm going to put my trust in you. I don't trust you,
so I'm going to act like I do, until I do."

Furthermore, Brennan Manning argues that authentic discipleship to Jesus is not defined by the one who reads his Bible religiously, goes to church services often, or even loves well. Rather,
authentic discipleship is marked by childlike surrender in trust to

Jesus with one's entire life.[25] The abiding life will cause us to trust Jesus ruthlessly with our lives- in action. And as we trust Jesus with our entire lives, as well as the resulting fruit, we're able to offer thanksgiving to the Lord for both the beautiful and the dreadful. Gratitude becomes our reality, knowing the Lord is using all of life to shape our likeness to his, even if we don't understand.

Surrender

The language of surrender is often talked of in Church circles, but has it become so cliché that it's lost its meaning? What does it actually mean to surrender our lives to Jesus? You may have heard teachings of "hoisting the white flag" or "placing your life at the altar," but this helps little if we end up with no application. I have therefore attempted to come up with ways to approach the issue of surrender, since it proves to be a vital action for the abiding life.

I'd like to offer two approaches to surrender, both mirroring a three-strand rope. Firstly, surrender always includes God's way, God's time, and God's purposes. The problem is that we're often only content with handing over two of the three strands. "God, I'm fine with however you want to work in my life and however long this process will take, but this better end up with an outcome I agree with." Or, "God, to you be the glory, and I'll wait as long as I need, but can you make sure this goes down in the most convenient way for me?" Or, "God, I will surrender how this turns out and the way you want to get there, but I'm going to wait a little longer before I'm obedient to you."

A life surrendered to God does not demand a say in what needs to be done, when it needs to happen, and why it is happening, because it accepts that we are not in charge; the vinedresser is. This is surrender: his way, his time, his purposes.

---

25 Brennan Manning, *Ruthless Trust: The Ragamuffin's Path to God*, 4.

The second practical aspect of surrender for me includes referring back to the Triangle. If you're ever confused about how to surrender your life to Christ in a given day, surrender to him the three elements of the Triangle: the actions of people in your life, the way these people think and feel about you, and how the situations and circumstances in your life will turn out. These three strands will entice us to grasp at them, but as long as we're grasping, we're not surrendering. Surrender freely expresses, "Jesus, I hand to you this day how others will choose to live, how others will choose to view me, and the results of the circumstances in my life." Not to mention, the tighter we grasp, the less we can hold. Jesus calls us to a posture of open palms.

Furthermore, in my mind, if we choose not to line up with his purposes in his way in his time, and surrender the actions of others, the thoughts and feelings of others, and the outcomes of the situations in our lives, whatever we are doing, it should not be labeled "surrender;" and it's probably falling short of abiding as well.

Waiting For Feelings

In the near future, each one of us will be tempted to delay surrendering our lives to Jesus until we feel the time is right. Maybe you find yourself in this mindset currently. The problem is for most of us, feelings are bad gauges for decision-making.

To illustrate, I'd like to push back on the notion that everyone's voice matters. "Everyone has an opinion, and because every person matters, every opinion matters." This idea has never been so widely accepted as it is today, and I think it is dead wrong.

If you were having financial trouble or were looking into investment options, would you ask advice from the person with large amounts of debt, no savings, and who has not proven himself trustworthy with money? Absolutely not. If you were thinking of attempting to lose weight and choose a healthier lifestyle, would you ask advice from the obese individual who never works out and frequently has a Twinkie on him? Absolutely not. Why? While every person matters, not every voice is equal. Over time, some voices have proven themselves more trustworthy than others, and these are the ones from which we should be taking advice.

Similarly, our feelings may be as dependable as a bankrupt Twinkie man. We should, consequently, at least consider that maybe our feelings have not been properly trained; that if our feelings have not proven themselves trustworthy over time, maybe they aren't.

Eugene Peterson argues that by changing our behavior, we can change our feelings; that we can act ourselves into a new way of being. Therefore, we should find the right things to do, be disciplined regarding the actions, and the feelings will eventually follow.[26] Most likely, the majority of us will not feel like surrendering our lives to God. Why? Because it's a decision to offer up control, and this cuts at the center of who we are as souls. It is a decision to choose humility, brokenness, and powerlessness. This will not come naturally, so we need to take advice from the voice that has proven itself trustworthy over time: Jesus's. And his instruction is a life of abiding surrender.

I will admit, pruning sucks. And surrender during pruning is a challenge to the greatest of saints. Pruning seems to strip and rip us apart at the deepest places we know ourselves. But surrender during pruning is precisely what prepares us for fruit.

Gary Thomas suggests: "It helps when we view our struggles in light of what they provide for us spiritually rather than in light of what they take from us emotionally."[27] Like a moth attempting freedom from its cocoon, beauty emerges from struggle. Similarly, *our redemption takes place as we go through difficulties, not around them.*

---

26 Eugene Peterson, *A Long Obedience in the Same Direction: Discipleship in an Instant Society*, 194-195.

27 Gary Thomas, *Sacred Marriage* (Grand Rapids, MI: Zondervan, 2000), 133.

What I want to avoid arguing here, though, is the idea that suffering teaches; because it doesn't. If suffering alone taught, everyone would be wise, because everyone suffers in some way or another. But if through our suffering we can muster up the courage to exhale mourning, trust, and vulnerability, our lives can be significantly enlarged. Ultimately, pain and suffering do not have to narrow us. Through grace and the help of the Spirit of Jesus, pain and suffering can be seeds that release us into wholeness.

Whatever Is Not You

They say Michelangelo was asked about his method for sculpting the statue of David. His reply was that he saw in the untouched marble stone the perfectly sculpted statue as though it existed. His task, then, was to chip away anything that was not David.

In the same way, the Father is pruning off of you whatever is not you, and in doing so he's giving you greater power to bear more and superior fruit. Even more so, he's giving you greater power to bear the image of his Son: the true vine.

Pruning hurts, but as Eugene Peterson writes, "Faith develops out of the most difficult aspects of our existence, not the easiest."[28] God's intent for our lives is not mere comfort. Aligning our hearts with his confesses we want him to be glorified more than we want to enjoy life. God is glorified by healthy fruit, and healthy fruit happens by pruning.

My prayer for you is that you would allow the vinedresser to do what he does best. Whether or not his pruning has been, or is currently, comfortable for you, his cleaning and pruning of you is purposed for the most good. He desires union and intimacy with you, and he knows it is possible by cleaning off whatever is not you. I pray for courage in you to respond appropriately: in worship and

---

28 Eugene H. Peterson, *A Long Obedience in the Same Direction: Discipleship in an Instant Society*, 79.

thanksgiving because the vinedresser is proficient at his job. You can trust him. And if you currently do not trust him, commit to *putting* your trust in him until the trust develops.

I think back through all my years of church life, through all the God-honoring conversations I've had, sermons I have listened to, retreats I have gone on, and cannot help but recall a phrase I've heard repeated over and over and over. An echo that lingers in my soul, as if it were a thread holding the years together. It's simple: "God is faithful."

How many times I have heard this phrase, and most often by the older folks- "God is faithful." I am genuinely intrigued by how many of the saints hold dear to this truth. "God is faithful." Maybe they have something figured out that most of us have yet to discover. My guess is, the older Christians alive today, on whose worn shoulders we stand, have had their faith tested, their trust in Jesus confirmed, and have come out the end of many dark tunnels with a life-changing truth resounding in their hearts: "God is faithful; he will not fail us."

No matter how rocky your situation appears, "God is faithful."

No matter how looming the dark may be in the valley of the shadow of death, "God is faithful."

No matter how unmanageable life presents itself, "God is faithful."

No matter how crushing the abiding life may be for you, "God is faithful." He is worthy of our trust and worship always.

I'm not sure I can sum up this chapter any better than by bringing attention to the thoughts of the late, great Henri Nouwen. May this be our worldview, our existence, and the paradigm that marks the drumbeat of our lives as we abide in Jesus, the true vine:

> "To be grateful for the good things that happen in our lives
> is easy, but to be grateful for all of our lives- the good as
> well as the bad, the moments of joy as well as the moments

of sorrow, the successions as well as the failures, the rewards as well as the rejections- that requires hard spiritual
work. Still, we are only grateful people when we can say
thank you to all that has brought us to the present moment. As long as we keep dividing our lives between events
and people we would like to remember and those we would
rather forget, we cannot claim the fullness of our beings as
a gift of God to be grateful for. Let's not be afraid to look
at everything that has brought us to where we are now and
trust that we will soon see in it the guiding hand of a loving
God."[29]

"Every branch in Me that does not bear fruit
He takes away; and every branch that bears fruit,
He prunes it so that it may bear more fruit."
~JOHN 15:2

---

29 Brennan Manning, *Ruthless Trust: The Ragamuffin's Path to God*, 31.

Chapter 3
Questions For Personal Reflection and/or
Small Group Discussion

1. Is there anything in your life God has asked you to surrender that you have yet to lay down? Also, is there anything you can identify that if God asked for it, you could not release it to him?

2. What area(s) of your life have you been attempting to work through or fix on your own? What person or people can you invite into it?

3. Currently, do you desire God's plans for your life more than your preferred outcome for your life?

4. When difficult/painful experiences occur in your life, where do you usually wind up in relation to God:
angry and stressed, uncomfortably trusting, or broken but thankful?

CHAPTER 4.1

ASK WHATEVER YOU WISH
-FIRST BUTTON, FIRST HOLE-

"If you abide in Me, and My words abide in you,
ask whatever you wish and it will be done for you."
~JOHN 15:7

"Lift up your heart to God with a humble impulse of love,
and have himself as your aim, not any of his goods."[30]
AUTHOR OF THE CLOUD OF UNKNOWING

Lies Like Santa Claus

Certain lies have become socially acceptable in our culture; some even encouraged. Take Santa Claus for example: a large, jolly man in red who squeezes down chimneys to deliver gifts for good kids on Christmas Eve. Even though he has become an inspiring and even nostalgic character throughout the world, I find it a little it creepy that a fat guy supposedly sneaks into our homes once a year. Nevertheless, think for a moment about the fact that countless adults join in the annual Christmas

---

30 *The Cloud of Unknowing*, 10.

conspiracy. For good or bad, each winter, adults all over the world lie to children.

Now, it's not the lying itself that attracts my attention. What perks my interest is watching the adults lie. I find it amusing listening to adults make up stories of how they've seen reindeer, how they caught Santa on a roof, or how he eats their cookies by the fire each year. I also enjoy watching adults watch other adults in their lies; all the while, most of us are thinking the same thing: "We all know it's not true, and you don't believe the words coming out of your mouth." The fact is, adults do not believe in Santa Claus, but when they're around kids they play the part.

Now, with Santa, maybe no harm no foul; but what about with Jesus? One of Jesus's bewildering statements comes specifically to mind for me: "If you abide in Me, and My words abide in you, ask whatever you wish and it will be done for you."[31] Maybe you've quoted, possibly even memorized this verse or ones like it, but I wonder if you actually believe it.

I have sat in many church services listening to preachers exclaim with conviction, "Ask anything in the name of Jesus in faith and it will be done for you!" Immediate responses of, "Yes!" and "Amen!" are projected from the mouths of believers, but do their hearts convey a different message? I wonder how many Christians in those moments are thinking: "I would love for that Scripture to be true in my life, but I've asked many things in the name of Jesus in faith and they didn't happen." I also wonder how many preachers encourage people to have the faith of a mustard seed in order to move mountains, in hopes that it may work in someone else's life because it isn't in their own.

And then the irrational reflections flood in: "Maybe I didn't have enough faith. Maybe I have sin in my life the Lord is unpleased with. Maybe I didn't say the right words in my prayer." I'm sorry but faith enough to ask *is* the faith of a mustard seed.

---

31 John 15:7

In fact, we even see in Scripture that the faith of another person can be enough for one's own healing and salvation.[32] God also answers prayers regularly for people who have 100 times more sin in their lives than you. Don't discredit your prayers because of your past failures; God doesn't. Moreover, God does not work from a spell book that demands precision of word choice, cadence of pronouncement, or number of times it is prayed. There are wrong ways to pray, but there is no right way. Prayer is simply relationship and conversation with God, which means we should be praying what is in us, not what we think is supposed to be in us.

So what is Jesus getting at then? Why is it that we've prayed for good and unselfish outcomes, maybe purposed for the glory of God, and maybe they were even prayers that lined up with Scripture, yet we still ended up with results contrary to what we intended? I want to address these questions, but it would do us well to first explore the concept of our Christian walk as a journey of union with God.

Transforming Union

Have you ever noticed the nature of Jesus's conversations with the Father as expressed in the gospels? It looks quite different than most Christians' prayer requests. In fact, if you pay close attention you will notice he doesn't ask for much from the Father during his earthly ministry. When he turns water into wine, he tells the servants to fill jars with water and then take the newly made wine to the headwaiter. When he feeds 5,000 men and their families, he gives thanks and breaks the bread. When he heals ten lepers, they ask for mercy and he tells them to show themselves to the priests. He spits on a blind man's eyes for healing, tells a little dead girl to get up, and replaces a severed ear onto a man's head. Jesus's word

---

32 Mark 2:1-12

choice in prayer evidently did not exist by persuading the Father to perform miracles for him.

Some of you may be thinking by now: "Well, he was God; he didn't have to pray to himself." I encourage you, however, to not quickly forget that he was just as human as you and me. While in Jesus's day they underestimated his divinity, today we tend to underestimate his humanity. Jesus's sweaty armpits stunk; when he fell down, his knees bled. Jesus, in his humanity, even exemplified his lack of omniscience- he limited his own divine power when leaving heaven's glory.[33] He was a human being standing humbly before the Father just like every one of us. Why, then, did he rarely/never ask from the Father like we do? Or maybe we should be asking the opposite: why do we continually ask like Jesus did not?

When questions like these are brought up, I'm immediately drawn to John 17:22-23, where Jesus reveals the deep intentions of his heart to the Father: "The glory which You have given Me I have given to them, that they may be one, just as We are one; I in them and You in Me, that they may be perfected in unity, so that the world may know that You sent Me, and loved them, even as You have loved Me."

Jesus rarely/never asked of the Father because he was one with the Father; not merely because he was God, but because in his humanness he learned how to abide in the love of the Father to the point where he and the Father became one. His heart, his passions, and his spirit were so in line with the Father's that he didn't need to ask what the Father wanted. He knew.

This is precisely why Jesus commanded his disciples to abide in him. He did not merely want more miracles or bigger crowds to follow him. In fact, he claimed that his followers would do greater things than he did in his own life and ministry.[34] What Jesus truly anticipated for those who would devote their lives to him was

33 Philippians 2:5-11
34 John 14:12

to ultimately become one with the Father as he was one with the Father. Therefore, because Jesus is the way, the road, and the door to relationship with the Father, our unity with the Father is entirely dependent upon our commitment to abiding in Jesus.

The classical understanding of Christianity is one of a pilgrimage- a lifelong training. Candidly, I'm quite sick of reading books and hearing sermons about five easy steps that will solve your problems and make you a better Christian tomorrow. But this is largely reflective of our culture. We're taught that we can receive quality without discipline, but excellence and depth do not happen instantly.

I think to the greatness that is coffee. More than a mere hobby, coffee is a passion of mine. And not for the caffeine. I savor the craft of brewing specialty coffee. Because of the amount of research, practice, and experimenting I've done with brewing coffee, I can make a cup that competes with most specialty coffee shops. Whether a quality pourover like the Chemex or v60, a mean cup from a stovetop Mokapot, or a rich Turkish coffee from an ibrik, there's not an instant coffee maker that can keep up with what I make. The reason: *the good stuff in life takes time; and so it goes with God.*

Part of our Christian journey will include a radical shift in paradigm, calling us beyond knowing about Christ, into a patient and drawn-out union with him. We soon discover that we have been searching for God in every place imaginable except the one place he is most profoundly present: our own souls. When we muster the courage to journey into the unknown abyss within, transformation is offered as a gift of God's grace rather than the outcome of our own effort. Here, trying turns into yielding. Robert Mulholland Jr. notes that this type of union is a truly humbling reality because we finally grasp that there is nothing we can do to transform our likeness to Christ's except consent that work to the Spirit in us. We can accept it, but in no way can we cause union with God.[35]

---

35 M. Robert Mulholland Jr., *Invitation to a Journey: A Road Map for Spiritual Formation*, 97.

Much has been written on the idea of transforming union with Christ, and the majority of what I have found on this topic has been in the context of a life of contemplation. Thomas Keating is one of my "go-to's" regarding the contemplative life. He writes: "The contemplative life is the abiding state of divine union, in which one is habitually and continuously moved both in prayer and action by the Spirit."[36] For Keating, divine union is the unrealized goal of all Christians- whether they know it yet or not.

Keating similarly writes that transformation is completely God's work. "We can't do anything to make it happen. We can only prevent it from happening."[37] Therefore, the consent of our will is a discipline in which we must be well practiced. This brings to mind David's humble invitation to Yahweh in Psalm 139: "Search me, O God, and know my heart; try me and know my anxious thoughts; and see if there be any hurtful way in me, and lead me in the everlasting way."[38]

Thomas Merton is another distinguished advocate for the contemplative life. He has helped me immensely in grasping the ungraspable nature of our God. Merton writes, "Unless He utters Himself in you, speaks His own name in the center of your soul, you will no more know Him than a stone knows the ground upon which it rests in its inertia."[39] The contemplative life leans into the notion that God cannot be understood except by himself. Therefore, if we are to understand him, we must in some way be transformed into him, by him, knowing God only as he knows himself.

This is the transforming union about which Jesus prayed to his Father. The Father longs to be known by his children, but this kind

---

36 Thomas Keating, *Open Mind, Open Heart*, 12.

37 Thomas Keating, *Open Mind, Open Heart*, 16.

38 Psalm 139:23-24

39 Thomas Merton, *New Seeds of Contemplation*, 39.

of knowing is only possible by his children becoming him- which can only happen through a life of abiding in the vine.

Another way I've heard this transforming union described is through a process of our love being renewed. We all start in life with an immature love: *loving ourselves for ourselves*. We take care of, protect, and provide for ourselves because we believe the world revolves around us. Eventually we encounter God, and our love is morphed into a prudent love: *loving God for ourselves*. We learn to love him, but mostly for the blessings he brings to our lives, or possibly to avoid an eternity in hell. The next season brings a transformation to an unselfish love: *loving God for God*. In this stage, we move from desiring the provisions of God to desiring the God who provides; we love God for who he is, independent of what he can offer us. Lastly is perfect love: *loving ourselves for God*.

The logic behind concluding with the love of self for God is found in the great commandment. If we have not learned to love God well, we will not love self well, and therefore will have no capacity to love others for who they are. Not loving yourself will eventually do your neighbors harm. Unfortunately we have the ability to love our neighbors as a way of validating who we are- loving neighbor for love of self. God's desire is to guide us from loving him well, to loving self well, to loving neighbor well.

As you can see, the process of internal transformation culminates outwardly. Mulholland writes it this way: "Note especially the purpose or focus of the transforming union: 'that they also may be in us, so that the world may believe… that they may become perfectly one, so that the world may know that you have sent me.' Wholeness in Christ, transforming union, is for the sake of others."[40]

Hence, the point: outward love of neighbor will tend toward dysfunction without an internal transformation of one's love by

---

40 M. Robert Mulholland Jr., *Invitation to a Journey: A Road Map for Spiritual Formation*, 100.

Love himself. To merely love outwardly like Christ did is to fail, because even a Pharisee can figure this out in time. *The definitive goal of the abiding life is the consent of our will to the Father, the vine-dresser, so our outward love is birthed from a transformed heart.* Love, then, becomes fertile soil for transforming union with God.

First Button, First Hole

The illustration: when I wake up in the morning and put on a button-up shirt, I normally start with the bottom button and work my way up to the top. However, if I stick the first button in the second hole, it doesn't really matter how many I get right after that- the shirt is going to sit crooked. If I want the shirt to sit straight on me, I need to put the first button in the first hole.

Because this chapter centers on union with Christ, I want to come back once more to the intimacy factor in abiding. *Intimacy with Jesus is the first button in the first hole of Christianity.* If we don't get this right, it doesn't really matter what else we get right. Everything will sit crooked. Unfortunately, what we think we're supposed to accomplish *for* God frequently distracts us from intimacy *with* him, which in reality, is what we're supposed to accomplish.

The Christian message is that our Creator has invited us into eternal life, but for many, eternal life is something waiting to be experienced after death. Dallas Willard suggested otherwise: "The only description of eternal life found in the words we have from Jesus is 'This is eternal life, that they [his disciples] may know you, the only real God, and Jesus the anointed, whom you have sent" (John 17:3). This may sound to us like 'mere head knowledge.' But the biblical 'know' always refers to an intimate, personal, interactive relationship."[41] *Eternal life is not getting to heaven when we die. Eternal life is living intimately with Jesus now.*

---

41 Dallas Willard, *The Divine Conspiracy: Rediscovering Our Hidden Life In God*, 49.

This should bring new perspective to probably the most over-used, misunderstood verse in all of Scripture- John 3:16. For God so loved the world that he gave his only Son to die, that whoever would believe in him would not perish but have *intimacy with God.* As Christians, as abiders, *where we are headed is not a destination; it's a union.*

But this idea is widely miscalculated, right? Christians love to use the language of the promised land. Figuratively speaking, "I'm in slavery, but God is leading me to the promised land." Or, "I'm in the desert, but God is leading me to the promised land he prepared for me." Determination sets in, and eyes fix on the destination. But have you ever looked into why God took the Children of Israel out of Egypt? I missed it for years. God had Moses lead the Children of Israel out of Egypt and into the desert, not to get to the promised land. He did it so they would find him in the desert.

In Exodus 7, God instructs Moses: "Tell Pharaoh, 'God sent me to tell you, Let my people go, *so that*, they may worship me in the desert.'"[42] God did not pull them out of slavery for a change in zip code; he freed them for intimacy with him in the desert.

We tend to think in terms of promised land, but if we're seeking the blessings of God over intimacy with the God who blesses, the abundant life will remain a blind spot. In fact, we're often more fond of the blessings Jesus offers than the cross he offers. We tend to orient our lives around "promised land," but we were created for intimacy, and promised land is intended to be a natural result of that intimacy. *Meaning, following Jesus is not about where you're going. It's about finding God where you are.*

We can also look to someone like the Apostle Paul. What a remarkable man of God with a list of astounding achievements.

---

42 Exodus 7:16

Incredible resume- one of the greatest in the history of the Church. Yet, in his letter to the Philippians he writes:

> "If someone else thinks they have reasons to put confidence in the flesh, I have more... But whatever were gains to me I now consider loss for the sake of Christ. What is more, I consider everything a loss because of the surpassing worth of knowing Christ Jesus my Lord, for whose sake I have lost all things. I consider them garbage, that I may gain Christ and be found in him..."[43]

Did you catch what he's doing here? The Apostle Paul: church planter extraordinaire; writer of much of the New Testament we read today; one of the greatest Christians of all time- if we don't give him the number one spot, he has to be on the top five list, right? This guy essentially says, "You want to compare resumes? I'll win. And when I hold my resume up against the mere reality of knowing Jesus, my accomplishments in comparison to intimacy with Jesus, everything I've done is garbage, even excrement." Paul intentionally wanted to communicate the stark contrast between the best he could accomplish, and the importance of intimacy with Jesus.

Therefore, and follow me here, if the Apostle Paul wanted to communicate that his best accomplishments were dung up against knowing Christ, what do you think he would say about your best accomplishments? I'll let your imagination play with that...

More than anything you can do for God, more than anything you can achieve for his Kingdom, the thing God wants most from you is intimacy with you. Intimacy is knowing and being known by another. Transparency. Vulnerability. This is what Jesus calls us to. Knowing him. Allowing ourselves to be known by him.

---

43 Philippians 3:4, 7-9

To take it a step further, our intentional and regular time with Jesus is not just for us. I think he is thrilled by the fact that we show up; overjoyed as we make space in our busy lives to be with him. And while I believe Jesus deeply longs for this, he is a gentleman. He will not force himself upon us. He graciously invites us into eternal life.

We were created entirely for intimacy. It is the first button in the first hole for the abiding life. If we miss this, we miss everything.

CHAPTER 4.2

ASK WHATEVER YOU WISH
-TO GOD BE THE GLORY-

> *"If you abide in Me, and My words abide in you,*
> *ask whatever you wish and it will be done for you."*
> ~JOHN 15:7

> *"Lift up your heart to God with a humble impulse of love,*
> *and have himself as your aim, not any of his goods."*[44]
> AUTHOR OF THE CLOUD OF UNKNOWING

Sneaky Jesus

Alright, let's get on to Jesus's "ask whatever you wish" statement. As we commit to abiding in Jesus, we will experience intimacy and oneness with him, and therefore, oneness with the Father. Thus, what the Father is passionate about, what he is disturbed over, what he burns for, and what he dreams of is transferred into our hearts. Over time, we notice that our desires look more and more like his. Our requests will, accordingly, be birthed from the Father's desires rather than from our own selfish, human cravings.

---

44 *The Cloud of Unknowing*, 10.

The Father yearns to transform your heart to his, so that everything you want is what he wants; that everything you ask for is everything he wanted in the first place. With requests, then, originating from the very heart of God, why would he not grant them? Why would he not act on the requests of those who long for the same things he does?

I use the phrase "sneaky Jesus" because the language he uses sounds like, "When you abide in me, you get whatever you want through your prayers," but what he really communicates is, "When you abide in me, the Father gets whatever he wants through your prayers."

Jesus's own life is an impressive model of this. Before he's arrested in the Garden of Gethsemane, Jesus asked the Father to take the cup from him- essentially asking if the cross could be avoided. But then he ends his request with, "… Nevertheless, your will be done." In a similar manner, I think we should ask for lots of things from the Father. Not just because he can give us what we want, but because he told us to ask for things- and to ask persistently, annoyingly, even audaciously. But like Jesus, we also need to learn to pray "… Nevertheless…"

We must understand the goal in prayer is not that we simply get what we want. The goal is that we get his heart. What I recommend is disciplining yourself in asking for his heart more than for situations and outcomes, so you can know *how* to pray in the first place.

I have unfortunately come to know Christians who seem to have Matthew 6:33 memorized in reverse, which would read: "Seek first all the other things you want, and his Kingdom and his righteousness will be added to you." Many of us need a paradigm shift when it comes to our prayer lives. God is not in the business of prospering and blessing what we put our hands to; he is a master surgeon performing heart transplants so we can participate with what he is putting his hands to. The abiding life aligns our hearts with God's so we're not simply doing our own thing and asking

God to bless it. As we grow in abiding, we grow in participating in what he is already up to in our lives.

To unravel this idea a bit further, I refer to one of my favorite theological terms: *perichoresis*. Theologians often use this word to help depict the relationship between Father, Son, and Spirit. *Perichoresis* describes God's moving in sync with himself, and may best be understood as a divine dance between the three persons of the Trinity.

Before eternity, the Father, Son, and Spirit have been swaying and weaving to the music of their love and service towards each other; colorfully choreographing past, present, and future in a rhythmic and mutual giving and receiving that elevates the others in the dance. And then astonishingly, they invite us into the dance as well.

The point to be made here is that before you entered the scene, God was delicately at work in what would become your life. God's dance was sowing grace, weaving shalom, and breathing love into your world long before you took a breath in it yourself. We do not initiate anything in this life. He has created for his purposes. He has given us the privilege of *joining* him in the renewal of all things- in joining our heavenly Father in the dance that will reconcile and redeem his entire creation back to him.

Contrary to what you may have been taught, *God does not want to give you the desires of your heart; he wants to replace your desires, your passions, your will with his so he can live out the desires of his heart through you.* I love the way John the Baptist worded it: "He must increase, but I must decrease."[45] Is this your "'raison d'etre;" your reason for existence? Because your prayer cannot be, "We must increase together." Either you are increasing or God is increasing in your life.

I also wonder if God does not answer our prayer requests how we intend at times because our prayers reflect a desire to not need

---

45 John 3:30

him in situations. For example, awhile back I asked God to increase my monthly income because finances were tight. I was living the frightening reality of a month-to-month paycheck, so I asked if he would change my circumstances so my finances would be more stable.

Now, not to say this prayer request was wrong, nor am I arguing that God does not want to stabilize our finances. But in this situation, God communicated to me with a commanding whisper: "Why would I answer a prayer to not need me as much as you currently do?" Essentially my request asked God to set me up to live in less faith; to make me self-sustainable. Looking back, I'm thankful he didn't provide more during that season. My trust in God was stretched, and I now have more faith in God, in part, because of that season of dependency on him.

The great and terrible truth is that there's nothing you can do to fix yourself. You are broken, dirty, and your absolute best is like filthy rags before the righteousness of God. In short, there is only one thing possible and one thing necessary for transforming union with God: the consent of your will to be transformed by him, in his way, in his time, and for his purposes. Precisely the abiding life. In time, if we let God change our hearts to his, we *will* get everything we want in prayer.

Decision-making for Transformation

Given that so much of this chapter has to do with the process of our transformation, I thought it appropriate to add in one more piece of the puzzle regarding how we participate with this process: decision-making.

I think back through the earlier decades of my life and wonder how many times I heard the phrase: "God has a plan for your life." Or, "You were born to accomplish big things for God." I think back to the times I've even said them myself. The idea that God has created and destined our lives to accomplish significant things for his Kingdom is familiar language in western Christian culture. And not that I necessarily disagree with it per se, but I do want to come at it from a complementary angle.

The problem with keeping "God's plan for our lives" at the forefront of our minds is that we end up directing our lives and making decisions from a foundation of what we believe God wants to accomplish through us. You may ask: "Isn't that exactly what the Christian life is all about?" In short: no, it's not. The Christian life is first and foremost about who we are and who we are becoming, and secondly about what will be done out of who we have become.

Many devoted Christians will make life-altering decisions because of what they believe God wants them to accomplish in life. And while their intentions may be virtuous, there is a better option: the experienced, devoted Christians will learn to make decisions out of who they believe God wants them to *become* in life. This option carries more weight because God is more interested in who you are becoming than what you will accomplish for him. The reason: *what you accomplish in life will result from the aftermath of who you will become.* If you simply chase accomplishing things for God, you may miss who he wants you to become, therefore missing what you are purposed to do for him.

Furthermore, this is where I think so many Christian leaders fall. They strive to undertake more for God than he is asking of them, sacrificing and serving beyond their capacity, ignoring their character along the way. Eventually the weight of their roles and authority becomes too much for their character to hold up and they self-destruct, destroying the influence, relationships, and responsibilities they're carrying. To be blunt, there's no need to waste your time serving God if you don't care to be transformed by him.

I would also like to add that the emphasis in the New Testament is on followers of Christ being responsive to the Spirit's work in us rather than starting projects we expect God to back up. We need to keep perspective here. I encourage you to lean into and *learn* into making decisions beyond setting yourself up for what God wants you to do. Rather than focus on what you should be accomplishing, focus on the posture of your heart; in doing so, you will accomplish what you need to. Whether our life choices involve a job, a local church, a significant other, or even how we spend our money, making decisions that set us up for *becoming* will create the environment for us to *accomplish* what Jesus wants us to.

To God be the Glory

Jesus told his disciples that the Father is glorified by large amounts of good fruit production. Which means we are ultimately moving towards the Father receiving glory from the way we live our lives, and even further, him receiving glory from the consequences of our lives- the fruit. If you've been around church life for any amount of time, the language of "bringing glory to God" is likely familiar territory for you. But precisely what are we after in bringing glory to God? What does it practically mean to bring glory to the Father?

To start, *glorify* means to bestow adoration or praise to something; to light up brilliantly, to be seen more clearly than before. My guess is that many of us could genuinely claim we want God to be clearly seen and known throughout the world. However, if we took an honest look at our motives, it's likely that many of us could also genuinely admit we want ourselves to be seen and known as well.

Christians are just as skilled in the world's games of promotion and authority as those wanting nothing to do with Jesus. Loads of Christians are concerned about church score boards, human applause, and external rewards. One of the greatest failures of our faith may be the absurd belief that our spiritual acts and virtues need to be advertised and known. The desperate efforts of religious people to broadcast themselves are a stunning revelation of their lack of abiding in the true vine. Abiding and fruit bearing brilliantly light up the name of God, not other names. Abiding leads us to hand over our public relations department entirely to the Father. In doing so, glory will more regularly go to him.

It could be argued that similar to Ptolemy's miscalculation of the physical universe (that the earth is the center of the universe), one of the central problems of humanity is that we think we're the center of the relational universe. Many of us are consciously and subconsciously raised to believe the entirety of creation revolves around us as individuals.

I liken it to being an extra in a movie or TV show. In fact, I had the opportunity to do "extra" work in the past. In one scene in particular, I was asked to walk from right to left in front of the camera. I was literally in the shot for one second. All you can see is my big, blurry head pass by because the focus was on the main characters farther back.

Now, hypothetical situation: let's say I encouraged all my friends to make sure they watched my episode the night it aired because I was going to be the main character in it. What do you think is going to happen after the show is over? Maybe even before the show is done? I'm likely going to receive a few phone calls and texts saying something to this extent: "I love you, but you're an idiot. You were not the main character in that show, and the episode was not even close to being about you. You weren't even a supporting role. You didn't even have any lines. We could barely even see your face in it. You were in the shot for a second!"

Likewise, and to be blunt, this life, this story is not about us. We are not the main characters. We're not even supporting roles. True, we play a part in the story, but it's a small one. As extras we are necessary, but in the grand narrative, our big, blurry heads are in the shot for one second. Hence, I presume *the less central we place ourselves in the story of what God is up to in humanity, the more freedom we give him to use us in that story.* God is not involved in our story. We have been invited into his, to join in his love affair with his beloved creation. Gratitude and thanksgiving should be our first response as he lets us join his family, and join in renewing all things back to himself through grace and love.

The unfortunate truth, however, is that we can abide and bear fruit, but then insist we get the credit and glory for it all. I like to take my cues, again, from John the Baptist on this one. He knew he was preparing the way for the Messiah, and when Jesus approached him one day, he actually sent his own disciples away to follow Jesus. What type of ego must have been laid down to send followers away to another teacher? Pointing to Jesus was John's destiny. Humility before the Messiah was the culmination of his life; he said he was not even worthy to tie Jesus's sandals.

It makes me think of a time I was at an Angels baseball game in Anaheim with my dad- it was actually a church event that many people from the church attended together. My dad and I were sitting in the back of the section our church friends were in. While those around us were enjoying watching the game and entertaining conversation with each other, my dad and I were having a blast chucking peanuts at our friends far below. Those friends we hit would look back with loving insults and smiles, yet a few peanuts hit people that weren't from the church. Strangers would look up in our direction, and what would we do? We looked behind us too. My dad and I got the biggest kick out of holding the back of our heads as if the rogue peanuts nailed us as well. We attempted to direct attention beyond us, even though we did the throwing.

As Christians, maybe even as the Church, we have become well versed in "chucking Kingdom peanuts." Many of us are efficient and skilled at getting stuff done for the Kingdom of God, and we even have a blast doing it, but then people look to us awaiting a response. Eyes turn toward us, curious about what we will say. How do you respond?

Transforming union is not about bringing attention to us. It is purely about bringing attention and glory to the Father. In fact, the more profound our transformation, the more profound our declaration should be of the one who transforms us. As Merton puts it: "The truer and more intense the light is, the less you see the glass."[46] The light of Christ burning in us does not reflect our image, but his. We do, however, get a choice in the matter. When we shine brilliantly, we can either boast in the long and tiring journey that led to our amazing works, we can revel in the goodness and greatness we possess, or we can grab the back of our heads and point to the One beyond us.

In his book *Just Walk Across the Room*, Bill Hybels notes that throughout the course of your life, you will give your life to something. Everyone will. Maybe to pleasure or possessions, to popularity or power; but always to something. True followers of Christ, however, will give themselves to pointing people to faith in Christ. "That is the highest and best use of a human life- to have it serve as a signpost that points people to God."[47] *Our assignment as abiders is not just bringing people to church; we are commissioned to bring people to Jesus.*

We should ask ourselves how much we're going out of our way to make sure Jesus's name is remembered over our own? Think of how many opportunities during a normal day you can easily direct public praise and glory to the Father. Think of how often a typical day brings occasions to visibly boast in the grace of Christ; of how the Spirit has blessed us with her presence and action again and again. We have more than enough opportunities in a day to boast in the love of God for us. Although we may claim our greatest

---

46 Thomas Merton, *New Seeds of Contemplation*, 189.

47 Bill Hybels, *Just Walk Across the Room: Simple Steps Pointing People to Faith*, 28-29.

desire is for God to receive glory, our actions can communicate another message.

So may we purpose our lives not only to bring glory to the Father through their fruit, but also to live committed to chucking Kingdom peanuts and never stop pointing to the One who made the peanuts.

> *"If you abide in Me, and My words abide in you,*
> *ask whatever you wish and it will be done for you."*
> **~JOHN 15:7**

Chapter 4
Questions For Personal Reflection and/or
Small Group Discussion

1. How would you, or possibly your closest friends, define your life: "loving yourself for yourself," "loving God for yourself," "loving God for God," or "loving yourself for God"?

2. What have been some prayers that did not turn out how you wanted? What do you think God may have been up to in not answering them the way you wanted?

3. What has been more of a focus for you of late: what you are accomplishing, or who you are becoming?

4. What are some regular and consistent ways your life can direct glory to God?

CHAPTER 5.1

THE ONE JESUS LOVES
-WHAT IS LOVE?-

> *"Just as the Father has loved Me,*
> *I have also loved you; abide in My love."*
> ~JOHN 15:9

> *"To say that I am made in the image of God*
> *is to say that love is the reason for my existence,*
> *for God is love."*[48]
> THOMAS MERTON

The Love of Christ

It was a seemingly average Saturday morning in Santa Monica. I went to the bank to pick up quarters for an afternoon of laundry, and as I walked back to my car, St. Monica's Catholic Church caught my eye. Catholic and Eastern Orthodox church buildings intrigue me, and since the large double doors on the front of the building were open, I decided to take a peek inside.

As I entered the doorway, the beauty of the room immediately captivated me. To be candid for a moment, I'm tired of the many

---

48 Thomas Merton, *New Seeds of Contemplation*, 60.

criticisms of the Catholic Church. Everything from the rigid legalism, to worshipping saints and statues, to Protestants distinguishing between Catholics and "Christians"- which doesn't even make sense because Catholics are Christian… Many people are simply afraid of what they don't know. It disturbs me that in ignorance regarding another's approach to Christ, the Church implodes on itself.

While each branch of the Christian Church (Protestant, Catholic, and Orthodox) has its own pitfalls (yes, we Protestants have ours too), each brings a distinct beauty to the body as well. I appreciate the Catholic approach offering a stout reverence for tradition and wonder of the senses. And I sure experienced it that Saturday morning. Ornate stained glass windows, vivid icons, intricate statues, the enormity of the room, the elaborate crucifix, even the smells took hold of me.

I started in the back left corner of the room, slowly working my way toward the front of the room, across the front, and finally toward the back right corner. The walk around the room probably took me a good twenty minutes, and just as I was ready to leave, my spiritual antennae went up; something deep inside me sensed I was supposed to take a seat in the back wooden pew. I figured, "I enjoy sitting in the quiet alone with Jesus. I might as well take advantage of this moment alone with God."

I quieted my heart and mind before him, making myself present to God since he was already present to me. I centered on how thankful I was to be alive, to be offered relationship with God, for the many blessings, graces, and mercies that have filled my life. And then my eyes set on the large crucifix.

One of the differences between most Protestant buildings in comparison to Catholic buildings is whether or not Jesus is still on the cross. Again, this is a point of frustration for me because in that moment I could hear the ridicule from some of my ignorant Protestant friends: "How can Catholics keep Jesus on the cross? Don't they know he rose from the dead Easter morning?" Personally, I don't think this is a matter of which is right, but rather, of allowing the implications of both symbols to transform our hearts.

Yes, Jesus did rise from the dead Easter morning. His demonstration of power over death and sin that day distributed life into all who would believe in him. However, the cross is the signature of Jesus. The cross is the crux of human history that gives life and meaning to all Jesus's followers would do in his name. The cross *is* Christianity.

For this reason, I appreciate the rich tradition of the Catholic Church in keeping Jesus on the cross. It reminds us not to move to the resurrection in haste. Sure, power over death is awesome, but it only makes sense in the context of love poured out.

Back to St. Monica's Church. This specific Saturday morning is one seared into my soul for eternity. As I admired the detail and craftsmanship of the crucifix, I thought through the Bible studies I've led, papers I've written, and sermons I've preached on crucifixion. I began contemplating the sacrifice of Christ, and soon following, a thought delicately washed over my mind that hadn't before: I wondered how I would ponder the cross if the one hanging on it were a good friend of mine, or a family member. What if Jesus was not the one hung with nails by his hands and feet? What if it was my closest friend? What if it was my mom? Tears filled my eyes. It's easier to make Jesus's sacrifice on the cross some objective, detached act in history by considering a distant, all-powerful God laid down his life for us. I mean, he's God; how difficult could it have been for him, really? But in this moment I processed it through the lens of a person murdered for me. And then the thought that sank to my gut like a brick: "Jesus, the man, was murdered for me."

I sank further into it. What if a good friend or family member laid down his or her life to be murdered for me? In real life, what if someone I deeply cared for was killed because of my mistakes? I answered myself rather quickly: "I would think of that person's sacrifice for me frequently. In fact, every day would be lived in honor of them. Not a day would go by without appreciating their love for me." But why have I made it any different for Jesus? Why is the cross something I've learned to save appreciation only for Good Friday and while taking communion?

I quickly found myself in a pool of newfound tears and emotion. I don't know why God chose this moment in this church building, but it was here the love of Christ for me was made tangible. Neither do I understand why it took twenty-something years for the weight of the cross to hit me, but it seemed to have twenty-something years of momentum behind it.

I think of the way John the beloved wrote of his relationship with Jesus. He repeatedly referred to himself in his gospel as "the disciple whom Jesus loved." I mean, how arrogant, right? What about the others? Why did John refer to himself this way? The reason: *he got it.* The only thing that truly matters in this life is the expression and acceptance of love from the person of Jesus. In St. Monica's Church, I was brought to my knees in sheer gratitude for the love of God for me in Christ Jesus. I finally realized I am the one for whom Jesus died. *I am the one Jesus loves.* And it is this love in which he invites us to abide.

The New Testament on Love

In Matthew 22 we read over a conversation Jesus had with some religious experts. They asked what he thought to be the greatest commandment in the Law. His response: "You shall love the Lord your God with all your heart, and with all your soul, and with all your mind. This is the great and foremost commandment. The second is like it, you shall love your neighbor as yourself. On these two commandments depend the whole Law and the Prophets."[49] Apparently for Jesus, if you miss these, you miss everything.

Jesus's thoughts on the Greatest Commandments express that our priority is to love the Lord God with every ounce of our beings. We were created entirely for wholly loving Yahweh our Maker. Thomas Merton writes that human beings have no other reason for being, except to be loved by God as our Creator and Redeemer, and to love him in return.[50] Abiding in God is the foundation to all that is and will be built from our lives. Loving him and sharing intimate relationship with him is our cornerstone; the solo "Jenga" block remaining at the bottom of the tower from which everything else finds balance.[51]

I remember back to a conversation with a friend who was describing his struggles with low self-esteem. Interestingly, the ways insecurity and self-doubt attempted to work its way out through his life were similar to the ways ego and arrogance attempt to work their way out through mine. How is it that egotism and a lack of self-worth manifest similarly in our lives? Playing with the dynamics of what these two extremes have in common led me to drawing up the diagram below.

---

49 Matthew 22: 37-40

50 Thomas Merton, *New Seeds of Contemplation*, 61.

51 If loving God is not your highest priority, a great way to begin or to continue growing in love of God is the three-fold abiding I cover in chapter 1.3: identity in, intimacy with, and obedience to him.

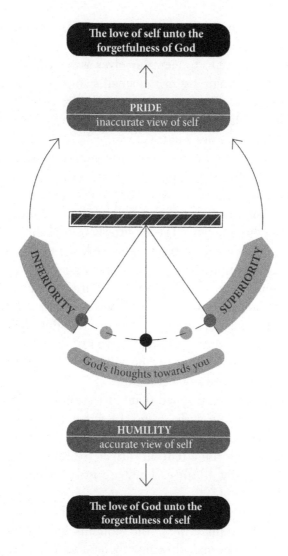

In the center of the diagram is a pendulum swing. The left side of the swing represents feelings of inferiority- thinking too low of self; the right side represents the opposite extreme, with feelings of superiority- thinking too high of self. What they both have in common, and how they interact with each other, is that they are (opposite) versions of pride- an inaccurate way of viewing self. Both extremes cause us to view ourselves as we aren't. What Jesus invites us into is lingering in the small swing area of God's true thoughts toward us- that we are beloved children of an affectionate Father; that he is head over heels for us; that we are loved just as we are. But what exactly are we?

Looking back to the origin of humanity in Genesis 2, we see God form man from the dust of the ground, breathing life into him, thereby making him a soul. Man does not have a soul; man is a soul. At the most basic level, he is a combination of physical and spiritual, dirt and deity. We are utterly remarkable and entirely replaceable, but we self-destruct when we lose sight of either side.

Clinging too tightly to our dirt, swaying into thoughts and feelings of inferiority, we forget that we are by nature, astonishing beings made by God. On the opposite extreme, clinging too tightly to our remarkability, swaying into thoughts and feelings of superiority, we forget the only reason we're astonishing is because the Creator says so. Either extreme will, therefore, eventually land us in pride- a mistaken self-perception.

Brennan Manning claimed that Christ's message of love is addressed both to those with a sense of self-importance and those crushed with a sense of self-worthlessness. "Both claim a godlike status because their full attention is riveted either on their prominence or their insignificance. They are isolated and alienated in their self-absorption." [52]

Moreover, the freedom from our compulsive narcissism requires a disciplined lingering in the thoughts and affection of God toward us; an intentional allowing of Christ to love us right where we are. In doing so, we will in time land in humility, which is an ability to view ourselves as we truly are. The product of humility, subsequently, is our true self.

---

52 Brennan Manning, *Abba's Child: The Cry of the Heart for Intimate Belonging*, 156.

Manning described our true self as an awareness that is unself-conscious, unpretentious, immersed in life, absorbed in the present moment, breathing in God as naturally as a fish swimming in water.[53] Here, our egocentric eyes are trained in relentless attention to Christ. We live out the freedom to be fully in the moment, present to God and the people in the moment, without impulse to present a counterfeit version of who we are to others. The true self rests in simply being; eyes ever fixed on our loving Savior.

Long term, then, pride and humility will produce in us either of two perspectives on life, as expressed by Augustine: the love of self unto the forgetfulness of God, or the love of God unto the forgetfulness of self.

To clarify, lingering in God's thoughts toward us is what escorts our hearts into humility. And it is humility that enables us to love God unto the forgetfulness of self. However, getting into the groove of abiding in the love of Christ can prove to be quite the arduous undertaking.

Once more, practically, what does this look like? How do we in practice, abide in the love of Christ? For me, two immediate responses come to mind: 1) spending enough time abiding in Christ (identity in, intimacy with, obedience to him) to actually give him space to tell us how he feels about us; 2) and then living as though we believe his love for us is genuine, until we actually believe his love for us is genuine.

In time we will learn to accept that we're not what we do, what we've accomplished, or what others say of us. We are the pride of our Father, who loves us beyond worthiness or unworthiness. As expressed in Romans 8, there is nothing in all of creation that can separate you from the love of God in Christ Jesus. Nothing in all of creation- literally everything that is not God- has the capacity to distance you from his love for you. Not even time. Not even free will. Not even your sin.

---

53 Brennan Manning, *Abba's Child: The Cry of the Heart for Intimate Belonging*, 49.

To be up front, lingering in this sway area of God's love for us is exceptionally demanding. While we were created for this love, our flesh fights in opposition and for control. And oh, that we may never be so foolish as to quantify the love of God for us based off our love for him. *More pleasing to Christ than any amount of prayers, discipline, or righteous living is that we believe he loves us.* His love yearns for our affection, if only we can find the courage to yield to its transforming work in us. All he asks is that we let him love us.

Moving forward, once we choose loving God (and being loved by him) as a lifestyle, we are then instructed to accept ourselves as God does so we may love ourselves as God does. Loving God well deposits in us the capability of viewing ourselves with God's eyes, with God's grace. Sin, insecurities, fear, and failures crumble as we find our identity solely in our son-ship or daughter-ship to Abba Father.

Something the Church must improve on is accenting Jesus's order for love. Many of us have been instructed to serve and love neighbor second to loving God, but Jesus was quite clear: love God, love self, love neighbor. The order is crucial.

Attempting to love ourselves fully before loving God fully is not even within our human capacity. We receive the gift of seeing ourselves as Christ sees us only via our ruthless pursuit of the love of God. So we abide. We lean into loving God with every ounce of our being- every thought, every decision, every relationship, every possession, laid before the Father as an act of love. Not only is this what we were created for, it also sets us up to be able to love and care for self as a byproduct. Grasping our belovedness is not something that can in fact be grasped; it is purely a gift of grace the Father offers to those who passionately seek his face.

Justin Buzzard once noted: "The gospel doesn't just free you from what other people think about you; it frees you from what you think of yourself." Many have heard of the unconditional love of God for them, but the way they actually think about themselves and the way they live out their belovedness does not line up with what they claim to be true about themselves. Brennan Manning's famous quote, "God loves you just as you are and not as you should be, because none of us are as we should be," seems just beyond believable.

It may be that the greatest hindrance to abundant, joy-filled life in Christ is our refusal to believe what he says about us. Out of our distorted view of self, insecurity takes root, and sin is born. Think of walking into a hall of distorted mirrors. Some mirrors make you look short and fat, others thin and tall, while others make your entire body bend. Sin has a way of distorting the mirrors we use to see ourselves, doubling us over in guilt, shame, and failing self-worth. Thankfully our God is exceptionally proficient at smoothing glass to help us look upon ourselves as he does. Abiding in the love of Christ for you places you in front of a straight and spotless mirror, allowing you to look upon yourself as you truly exist, so you have the option of loving yourself as Christ does.

You may ask simply, "But what does loving myself look like?" A good place to start is Paul's description of love in 1 Corinthians 13. While it may be an over-quoted passage at weddings, I'd like to offer a fresh approach to the text. Rather than reading it as a suggestion for how to love others, turn the passage toward yourself. If you would like to learn to love yourself well, *act* in love toward yourself the way Paul instructs in the chapter. Here's the list: be patient with yourself, be kind to yourself, don't envy another in comparison to yourself, don't boast about or dishonor yourself, don't get easily angered at yourself, keep no record of your own wrongs, rejoice in the truth about yourself, protect yourself, trust and hope in yourself, always persevere, and never give up on yourself. Moreover, this must be a chosen love, independent of feelings, because if we wait until we feel like loving ourselves as Paul's chapter advises, we may never act on it.

We are sinners far more than we realize, but we are loved far more than we realize. However, an unhealthy approach to either of these realities can push us into destructive extremes: the magnitude of our sin has the potential to drive us deep into shame and guilt, while God's unconditional love for us may give us false permission to take advantage of his unending grace. The crux of the gospel is where the gravity of our sin and the greatness of his love are held in tension, and the abiding life moves us along the path of greater understanding in both. The beauty is found in the balance of the two.

Furthermore, loving God and loving self becomes the foundation for loving others. The truth is, if you can't honor the divine DNA that moves through your blood, it will be impossible to see it or honor it in another. Our care for others is entirely dependent on our capacity for self-acceptance and self-affirmation.

Love of self, then, becomes the bridge between the love of God and the love of those around us, so we lean into it. William Menninger writes: "The spiritual masters have always insisted that the only authentic measure of our love for God is found in our love for one another."[54] Therefore, the extent to which we learn to love people will reveal the extent to which we have learned to love God.

According to the New Testament writers, you cannot claim to hate others and love God. Loving God and loving people, even loving enemy, are actually synonymous. Jesus made it clear that even horrible people can love their friends, but the love in which we are called to abide moves beyond those we deem lovable and into the realm of those completely undeserving.

Teresa of Avila put it this way: "The more advanced you are in love for neighbor, the more advanced you will be in love of God,

54 William A. Menninger, *The Loving Search for God: Contemplative Prayer and The Cloud of Unknowing*, 98.

for the love God has for us is so great that to repay us for our love for neighbor, He will in a thousand ways increase the love we have for Him... Beg our Lord to give you this perfect love of neighbor."[55]

Once more, the order for love must not be undervalued. Jesus was tremendously intentional: in loving God well, we are given the range to love self well, and in loving self well, we are given the range to love others well. If we choose not to love ourselves as God loves us, we will do harm to our neighbors. Our love will, in effect, develop out of our insecurities, our dysfunctions, our fears, and even our sin; but when our order of love is aligned with God's, everything effectively falls into place. Life literally hinges on love of God, love of self, and then love of neighbor.

John 13 is also a foundational chapter of Scripture concerning Jesus's understanding of love. He communicated to his disciples: "A new commandment I give to you, that you love one another, even as I have loved you, that you also love one another. By this all men will know that you are My disciples, if you have love for one another."[56]

The message of Jesus here is potent: the world would know of the disciples' love for Jesus by their love for each other. The identifying feature of their vertical love would be the demonstration of their radical horizontal love. Simply put, talk is cheap. Faith articulated through love is the only true expression of one's devotion to Christ.

The inescapable truth found in the life and message of Jesus is that his desire for the well-being and actions of his followers would be modeled after his own actions, principally through love. Keating adds that if the Spirit wanted more brilliant thoughts, she would call on the angels; that if God were looking for more

---

55 Teresa of Avila, *The Collected Works of St. Teresa of Avila: Volume 2- The Way of Perfection, Meditation on the Song of Songs, and The Interior Castle*, 351, 353.
56 John 13:34-35

geniuses, he would have created more of them. "What God is after from humans, according to the Judeo-Christian tradition, is our love."[57]

Interestingly enough, Jesus did not inform his disciples that the world would know of their *love* because of their *discipleship* to him; he said their *love* would communicate their *discipleship*. Jesus understood well the nature of discipleship to him. Identification to Christ is a fruit of love, not the reverse. Here, Jesus enlightens his disciples to the matter of priority: love must come first.

Furthermore, we see Paul write that without this love of which Christ spoke, anything else his followers would attempt would be in vain. Any one of us could speak in the tongues of men and angels, prophesy, have all knowledge, have all faith, be entirely generous in nature, and even die for Christ, but without love, none of it matters.[58] Love is entirely what you were created for, and is the purpose of the abiding life. His love is what draws us into the mystery of transformation. It is a redeeming work in the name and spirit of Christ that transforms the one loved as well as the lover; an all-consuming devotion to the Father that takes part in changing the world.

Agape

I've heard there are an unusually large number of words for *snow* in the Eskimo language. English, on the other hand, has less variety. Take the word *love* for example. We only have one word to define considerably different realities of love. I can claim to love coffee, reading, my dog, my job, my wife, and Jesus, in the same breath, using the same word for love. Therefore, while the New Testament uses the word *love* hundreds of times, we often interpret verses through the lenses of our personal experiences, which may

---

57 Thomas Keating, *Intimacy With God: An Introduction To Centering Prayer*, 69.
58 See 1 Corinthians 13:1-3.

differ significantly from what the writers of Scripture were intending to communicate.

In the language of the New Testament, there are four forms of love, two of which are used in Scripture, and one that is not used, but alluded to.

Storge was not used in the text, but communicates a type of love that binds families together. It is a love and affection a person has for a dependent, naturally occurring between parents and their children, and can exist between siblings as well.

Eros is a love alluded to in the New Testament, and communicates a romantic or sexual type of love. *Eros* love creates a desire to be near the target of the love; it's an emotional love.

Phileo love is used to describe a friendship developed between two or more people. It is a brotherly love creating a special interest in someone, frequently with focus on close association. Think of Philadelphia- the city of brotherly love.

Agape love is the purest form of love. It is a divine love; a love seeking only to give. It requires no payment or favor in response. It is not dependent on performance or environment. *Agape* is purely about the betterment of the other, seeking the other's welfare regardless of feelings. Emotion and affection have nothing to do with *agape*. In *agape*, there is no such thing as passive love. It is active. Chosen. A love mediated through the will. Here, it has become a decision of commitment; of covenant. *Agape* is virtuously unconditional.

Now, if you had to guess, what form of love do you think Jesus referred to when commanding his followers to love God, self, and neighbor? What form of love do you think Jesus told his followers would inform the world of their discipleship to him? What form of love do you think Paul used when writing of love to the church in Corinth? And what form of love do you think is used when proclaiming in 1 John that the very nature of God is love?[59] *Agape, agape, agape,* and yes, *agape.*

---

59 1 John 4:16

It is this love, this *agape* that God is and does. It is this *agape* in which he calls us to find our home; to abide. And once we have made the *agape* of Christ our home, we are beckoned to become sharers of this love. Jesus calls us from a position of receiving, to a position of offering, just as he does.

CHAPTER 5.2

THE ONE JESUS LOVES
-WHERE LOVE MEETS COMPASSION-

"Just as the Father has loved Me,
I have also loved you; abide in My love."
~JOHN 15:9

"To say that I am made in the image of God
is to say that love is the reason for my existence,
for God is love."[60]
THOMAS MERTON

My Journey of Identity

During the fall of 2009 my life was profoundly wrecked. What started out as my dreams come true quickly morphed into a death spiral of fear and loneliness. I was happily married to my junior-high sweetheart, and serving in my first ministry position as a youth pastor at a church I loved. I was literally living out my dreams. However, a little more than a year into what I thought was a happy marriage, my bubble was popped. My wife informed me that she was not sure about our marriage

---

60 Thomas Merton, *New Seeds of Contemplation*, 60.

anymore. She said she still loved me, but that she didn't know who she was, therefore questioning the validity of her commitment to me. I was given a choice: either she divorces me, or we separate in order to give her space to find herself. I chose the separation. As if this was not the worst news I had ever received, I was fired from my job that month as well. It was easily the worst month of my life.

I remember driving to Carlsbad one afternoon and walking along the beach until I found some cliffs overlooking the ocean. I settled down with only my Bible and a copy of *Abba's Child* in hand, and proceeded to tell God: "I don't know who I am anymore. Everything I thought I was and knew is gone. The places where I thought I had some amount of control have slipped through my fingers like the sand on which I sit. Lord, I'm not moving from this cliff until you give me some direction; and if that means three days, well then, I guess I'm sitting here for three days." Knowing Jesus heard my cry, I sank down into the center of my soul, grew still, and waited for the Savior's voice.

Since my youth, I have been sensitive to the leading of the Spirit through thoughts, urgings, and promptings, but I can probably only count on two hands the number of times I believe God has clearly spoken to me. I don't mean in an audible voice; rather, a deep knowing that the Creator is going out of his way to communicate something very specific to me in a moment. This was one of those moments.

After about ten minutes of stillness, God spoke to my heart in a deafening silence: "Today you came seeking guidance, but you won't be getting any. You came here seeking direction regarding what you are to do with your life. Instead, I want you to learn to be loved."

I responded back rather quickly: "What do you mean *learn to be loved*? I know what your love is. I've been born and bred for this. My mom went into labor with me in a youth group meeting! I've been in church my entire life. I am a pastor's kid. I have a degree in ministry, and have been a pastor for some time now. If anyone gets your love, it's me!"

God gave some space for silence, maybe for dramatic effect, then spoke words that shook my core: "You get my love in theory, but you've never drowned in it." The statement collided with my soul like a wrecking ball. More space for silence came, and then it clicked. At the moment I was watching surfers glide across the top of the waves. I realized I had similarly learned to ride on top of God's love; to stand, to maneuver some cool tricks, and to draw attention to myself in all of it, but I sensed that God desired something different from me- to choose to fall off my board, sink into the dark, cold water, and breathe it in. In that moment he said, "This is going to be painful and uncomfortable, but it will forever change you if you allow it."

A journey of identity ensued. The Lord drew me to himself in ways I had never experienced. He revealed to me that I am not the sum of my accomplishments; I am not my job title, a family member to any man or woman, or the amount of material possessions I have attained. I am defined not by doing, but from my being, created in and with the *imago Dei*. I am simply and profoundly a child of my Abba; a beloved son of the King of the universe, whose worth and value have been determined in eternity, before I even existed.

While these revelations sound lovely on paper, this actual journey I trekked was the darkest and loneliest of my life. I contacted my wife after a one-month separation, hoping she was ready to come home. She wasn't. Two months went by. Three months. Six months. A year. I remember sitting at my desk one day crying to the Lord, "This is not fair. I'm a good husband. I don't deserve this." The response I received almost knocked the wind out of me: "How do you think I feel, Josh? The Church is my runaway bride. Each day I invite you back into my arms and you continue to fail me. You continue to flee my embrace. Yet how do I respond? In grace. Mercy. Space. Always in love. And that is exactly what I'm asking of you now."

I committed to the Lord that day that I would never speak ill of my wife. That I would not belittle or pressure her, but attempt to treat her as Jesus would if he married her and she left him. I resolved in my heart to do the right thing, to treat her as I promised in my vows, and I was hoping deep down it would save my marriage.

It didn't. After a year and a half separation, we both knew the marriage was over. We filed for divorce and the marriage breathed its last breath.

I've heard it said we don't grow from our mistakes; we only grow from the ones we reflect on. For years I blamed my previous wife in my heart, denying all the places in our marriage I was selfish, arrogant, and anything but a servant. But as I reflected on the past, truly reflected with the help of the Holy Spirit, I concluded that our failed marriage was not her fault. Marriage is a two-way street. We failed each other. I'm finally able to admit I could have done much more before we even found ourselves in the separation. My active love for my previous wife did not resemble the example of Christ's love for his bride; in fact, far from it. I share responsibility for the failure of our relationship.

I also resolved to embrace, rather than hide from, this most trying time of my life. I knew Jesus was not surprised by the failure of my marriage, and that he had some form of redemption in mind. Zooming out from my situation for a second, I think Jesus intends to regularly work on our hearts through difficult circumstances, but if we're not paying attention to what he's up to, we miss it, requiring us to come back to another difficult circumstance later to grasp what he was trying to transform in us the first time. We regrettably end up circling a mountain multiple times before we decide to climb it. Consequently, I figured I would attempt as best I could to abide in Christ, in hopes of him bringing clarity to what he was up to in my life, so I could avoid wasting what I was going through.

While I hoped this season would transition out quickly, it didn't. My new reality was a shadowy despair. One I would not wish on my worst enemy, but it's also one I would not trade for the world. I chose not to waste this pruning. I committed to Christ that I would find his love in the dark, but I was pleasantly surprised. His love found me there. I looked my pain, my hurt, my wound in the face and clung to Christ with all I had. I jumped on the back of that dragon and rode it all the way to the bottom of the pit. And what did I discover down there? All that remained was Jesus. In the darkness I encountered the tremendous gift of Jesus's with-ness. He had been present to me all along.

I learned many things from that season, but what I grew most from was the identity lesson. It proved to be one of the more valuable I've ever learned. I realized that Jesus invites us to root our identity in him, but we are easily distracted by our roles and assignments. Looking back, my heart was not in the wrong place. I was living for God, but I rooted my identity in what I did rather than who Jesus says I am. I understood and viewed myself as a husband and pastor, and then invited Jesus into these roles. While this may be genuinely God honoring, it ultimately is a misunderstanding of my identity. I am not a pastor. I am not a husband. I am a beloved child of a compassionate, heavenly Father who loves me tenderly and invites me to find my home, my life in his Son, Jesus.

When we root our identity in our roles, eventually the weight of these roles will crush us. Dad, friend, co-worker, dog-lover, barista, provider, sister, student... Whether or not we can admit it now, we don't have legs strong enough to carry the weight of these roles. In time they will crush us. Like a black hole, they will overwhelm and consume our understanding of ourselves.

This is precisely why Jesus invites us to root identity in him. His yoke is easy and his burden is light. Therefore, when our

137

identity is in Christ, he carries the weight of identity for us. Rather than our identity being found in our roles and attaching our "Jesus badge" onto them, freedom is possible through rooting ourselves in him, while he informs us how to enter back into those roles with new insight and power.

God ultimately wants us to stand face-to-face with whatever we're finding identity in outside of him and allow it to fall short. We may experience the death of a loved one, divorce, the loss of a job, a health problem, or even an inability to provide for our family. While these can be crushing times, we get to choose whether or not we come out changed.

It is a sad truth, but in my experience, most people don't have the courage to make this decision on the front side of being crushed. Looking back, I didn't. I say this as a warning and in love: *don't wait until you're crushed by competing identities to choose identity in Christ.* If it does happen, Jesus will compassionately scrape you out from beneath the wreckage and offer himself to you again, but we're given the choice on the front side.

You are not your job. You are not your roles. You are not the sum of your accomplishments. You are not an employee, a family member, or a friend. You are the beloved of God. *You are the one Jesus loves.* Root yourself in that reality. Abide in Jesus, your home, and allow him to give meaning to the roles and assignments over which he has given you responsibility.

Lastly, I want to remind you, maybe even inform you, our God is a redeeming God. As I have committed to root identity in Christ, he has given me back the roles of husband and pastor. I am now married to an astonishing woman, beautiful and talented. She is my star; the brightest soul I've known. And we share a healthy and Christ-honoring marriage together. She has also given us the most remarkable of daughters, through whom God is revealing himself to me with each new sunrise. Regarding pastoring, I now consider myself a wounded healer- as Henri

Nouwen so elegantly put it. Pastoring now flows out of who I am in Christ, and I find such joy in being offered the honor of walking life with people.

Simply put, life works as it was intended when identity is rooted in Christ. I hope my story can provide you a little courage and faith as you faithfully endure in your own journey of identity.

Barefoot Love

As I became more intensely found by the truth of my identity in Christ, the Spirit led me to Christ's challenging teaching on the least of these in Matthew 25. You should take some time to sit with this passage yourself, but the short version goes like this: When Jesus comes in glory with his angels he will sit on his throne before the nations and separate us. He will invite those on his right to come inherit the kingdom prepared for them by the Father because when he was hungry, they fed him. When he was thirsty they gave him drink. When he was a stranger, they invited him in. When he was naked, they clothed him. While sick and in prison, they visited him. The righteous will ask when any of these actions occurred. His response will be, the extent to which they did it to one of their brothers, even the least of these, they did it to him. Then the ones on his left will be told to depart from Christ because they never fed him, gave him drink, invited him in, clothed him, or visited him. These ones will ask when they rejected him. His response will be, the extent to which they denied the least of these, they denied him.

During the separation, I immersed myself in this passage for six months. Accordingly, I sensed the Lord invite me into a six-month journey without shoes to raise awareness for the unbelievable amount of people on the planet unable to afford, or lack access to, a pair of shoes. I went everywhere barefoot for six months: coffee shops, church gatherings, shopping, restaurants, concerts, golf, bathrooms, museums, Disneyland... As people realized I wasn't wearing shoes, they would ask about it and I'd inform them of the unfortunate reality for many individuals all over the world.

Now, I'd been part of a few awareness projects before this, but they left me unsatisfied because I wanted to do more than just raise awareness; I wanted to do more than merely provide people with a statistic. I brought this concern to the Lord, and he told me to do something about it. So I invited people into my journey. As my bare feet initiated conversations with strangers, I boldly asked them to give me shoes from their own closet, or even the ones they were wearing during our conversation.

I was astounded by how many people wanted to help. After the six months were over, a friend of mine took all the shoes I collected to multiple countries for people in need. Over those six months, with the help of many friends and strangers, I collected over 850 pairs of shoes that went out to the shoeless around the world.

While I was honored to have impacted the lives of hundreds, what I hold dearer is the transformation that took place *in* me during the six months. God informed me that how I choose to love people is how I choose to love him. My daily prayer became: "Jesus, break my heart over the things that break yours." What a dangerous prayer, and he began to answer it. He changed the way I saw people. The homeless man outside Albertson's, the guy with nicer clothes than mine pumping gas in his Range Rover, the 6 year-old competing with his mom's phone for her attention at Starbucks, the bank teller, barista, next-door neighbor, and even my own brother.

I realized I did not have to travel to India or China to find needy, disregarded people. They were on my street. Christ was in the flesh everywhere I went. Mother Teresa elegantly worded it this way: "I began to see Jesus all around me in *distressed disguise*." How I treated these people would be the expression of my love for Jesus.

Additionally, I recognized how often I confined the classification of "the least of these" to the homeless, orphaned, widowed, sick, hungry, abandoned, those in prison, and the like. While these *are* all Christ in the flesh, the least of these also include *the ones I least expect to be Christ* in front of me; which may in fact be myself.

God revealed to me how much Love himself has offered me; how much grace, forgiveness, and mercy have been lavished on me. I know I have been burned, hurt, abandoned, and sinned against by people, but the truth is, I have been the burner, hurter, abandoner, and sinner against others, and to Christ as well. Therefore, *I have no right not to offer others what Christ has offered me.* If I want to call myself a Christian- a little Christ- the extent to which I will allow myself to be emptied and poured out for others determines the extent to which my life will reflect Christ's.

Love in Theory

In Donald Miller's *Blue Like Jazz*, he tells a story of his college days when he and his friends built a confession booth for the non-Christians on campus. The difference with this booth was that the Christians sitting in the booth confessed sin to those who came in for confession. It was the followers of Christ who acknowledged they had failed to love. They told those who came into the booth that Jesus loved them, and they exclaimed with great sadness that in selfishness, they had misrepresented Jesus on their campus. Precisely love in action.

Now, while we may agree with this type of love in theory, it may not line up with the way we, in fact, choose to live our lives. Does our ruthless love of God lead us to an accurate understanding and living out of our belovedness? Does our belovedness produce an active love for our neighbors? Because attempting discipleship without love completely misses what Jesus was getting at. Attempting all the wondrous things Paul wrote of in 1 Corinthians

13, without drowning in the absolute love of God for us, completely misses the point of our discipleship to Jesus.

While most Christians are ready to enjoy the delights of love in eternity in heaven, many still cling tightly to resentments, animosities, and bitterness in the present here on earth. Merton once wrote: "Do not be too quick to assume that your enemy is an enemy of God just because he is your enemy. Perhaps he is your enemy precisely because he can find nothing in you that gives glory to God."[61] Likewise, so goes an old saying: "To live above with those you love: Undiluted glory. To live below with those you know: Quite another story."

It is all too easy to be sickened by the bullhorn guys holding bright yellow judgment signs at professional sporting events, but the seemingly insignificant and small acts of un-love push the world away from Jesus just the same. The attempt at being a Christian without abiding in the vine, without abiding in the love of Christ, is a ridiculous notion, and is precisely why the world thinks of the Church the way it does.

And I'd like to add here, believing Jesus is God, and believing he died for the sins of the world does not make a person a follower of Jesus. All the devils of hell believe Jesus is God and that he died for the sins of the world. What makes a person a follower of Jesus, is following Jesus. Mahatma Gandhi once expressed, "I like your Christ; I do not like your Christians. Your Christians are so unlike your Christ."

Sometimes to offer a little perspective to those I pastor, I ask questions like: "If every Christian in the world lived like you, loved like you, treated people the way you do, what type of world would we live in?" "If every Christian in the world lived out their faith how you do, what type of global Church would we have? How well would Christ be represented?" I encourage you to ask yourself these types of questions. Because if our attitudes, how we treat

---

61 Thomas Merton, *New Seeds of Contemplation*, 177.

people, and what we do in public and in secret fail to preach the gospel, what we choose to actually say about Jesus matters little.

You may be thinking: "What about the abusive husband? What about the so-called 'friend' who continually takes advantage of anyone offering an inch? What about the boss who sexually harasses anyone with breasts? What do we do about these people?" There is a big difference between self-sacrificial love and self-abusive love. In no way am I supporting the verbally and/or physically abused wife to stay in relationship with her husband, nor am I fighting for the relationship with the jerk of a friend or the perverted boss. Just because Christ longs for us to respond as he does, does not mean we should live intimately with everyone in our lives. There were many people with whom Jesus chose not to be intimate. Going to the cross for these people did not mean he chose to be pen pals with them too. Furthermore, love should draw healthy and respectful boundaries, and if someone crosses a line, love kindly chops off toes. This is one way in which we care for and love self in order to care for and love others.

Where Love Meets Compassion
I once heard a story about a man who stopped at the local pub after a long day of work. After downing a few beers, he proceeded home and got back in time for dinner. As he walked through the front door, his little daughter, who had peanut butter and jelly all over her face as well as a full diaper, rushed into his arms. Taken aback, he swung around to his wife and complained, "How the hell do you love something that smells like this?" Calmly she replied, "In the same way I love a husband who comes home stinking and drunk. You work at it."

There is a reason Jesus commanded his followers to love; more so, to love their enemies: because it does not come naturally. If you woke up every morning with a spontaneous yearning to pay the rent of the guy who mocks you at work, or mow the lawn of the woman who consistently claims to raise her children better than you, Jesus would not need to instruct you to love them.

Therefore, the starting point for love is obedience. You do it before you feel like doing it, because if you wait for the feelings, you may never end up doing anything to love. Ironically, in loving others, in loving enemies before the feelings come, the action of love may in fact create feelings of love. But in all truth, whether or not you feel like doing it, it has been commanded of us.

Jesus claimed if we love him, we will obey him. What ultimately defines the abiding life? We obey what he commanded; it has to start with obedience. Eventually, though, our love needs to move beyond obeying to actually catching the heart of Christ. We must in time transcend the command and be transformed by the heart behind the command.

I want to be particularly transparent here. Before I started writing this chapter on love, I sensed the Lord ask me to take a break from writing so he could initiate a heart check in me. In sitting with Christ, he revealed to me I was well versed at externally loving others in action, which is a great start, but my internal love for others was reserved for those I deemed worthy of that love. For example, I have overflowing compassion for those I believe to be in need of love: the homeless, the widows and orphans, children, new Christians, and even extremely selfish people who simply have not encountered the love of Christ. But what about people who should know better? What about those who could write this book better than me? The life-long Christian who gossips like a thirteen year-old; the pastor that "has no time" for people because he is busy building his church; the Christian leaders in positions of power who use their influence to dominate and manipulate others rather than elevate them.

Externally I have disciplined myself enough to love these people in action, but internally? That is quite a different story.

I take this moment for confession. For years I've looked on ones like these with judgment and contempt. My internal dialogue has continued to loop: "I cannot believe these people. Shame on them. They've been in the game for a long time; they should know better. They have no right to act like that; to treat people like that. I never would."

Then I thought to myself: "What if Jesus dialogued this way about me? Although he died for me- an external love- what if he thought about me the same way I have been thinking about these ones?" The truth is, my love has been completely conditional. It has been a love based off performance, which is as far from *agape* as it gets.

So I choose to come out of hiding. Who am I? I'm Josh Houston. A recovering narcissist. A divorcee. I'm proud, and arrogant, and insecure. Failure scares me. I've been fired. I judge others in my heart. I people-please. I self-promote. I lust. I compare myself against others. I'm selfish. I'm a control freak. I'm broken and fragile before the cross of Christ. I am a sinner in need of grace. I am the beloved of Christ, and a child of my heavenly Father. Thank God for love, because without it, I'm lost.

I currently find myself overwhelmed and in awe that God uses the broken to minister to the broken; that he would use a wounded servant like myself to minister to his body. Of late, I have been sitting at the foot of the cross, thanking Christ for his grace and mercy towards me. His love for me is without bounds, and he calls me into the depth of this love. Brennan once prayed, "Dear Jesus, if it's a fault for being too kind to a sinner, then it's a fault I learned from you." I long to be robustly outrageous with grace as Christ is.

But what made the love of Christ so powerful? Why did his active love carry so much weight? Again, it was not simply because he was God; he had to decide to *be* love just like we do.

What I've come to understand about Jesus is that his love had such eternal impacts because of his unfathomable compassion for those he ministered to. Christ's love was not a, "My dad told me to love you" kind of love, like a kid forced to apologize for smacking his brother in the back seat of the car. Jesus's love was one that burned like a holy acid in his belly.

Have you ever read the gospels and come across the words: "Jesus was moved with compassion"? Depending on the translation it may read Jesus felt pity, felt sorry, or his heart went out to a specific people. The word for "compassion" is used twelve times in the four gospels from the Greek verb *splagchnizomai*. Unfortunately, once again the English translation misses the profound physical and emotional flavor conveyed in the word.

As Brennan Manning used to teach so brilliantly, *Splagchnizomai* comes from the Greek, *splanxna*, communicating one's inward parts, especially the nobler entrails – the heart, lungs, liver, kidneys, and bowels. These parts gradually came to denote the seat of affections from which the strongest emotions like love and hatred arise.

Splagchnizomai can be translated as a relentless tenderness causing one to be moved from the bowels- meaning Jesus did not merely feel bad for people. Every time we see in Scripture that Jesus was moved with compassion, we must understand his gut was twisted, his heart ripped open, and the most vulnerable part of his soul revealed. He was literally pulled from his insides outward.

To take it a step further, *splagchnizomai* in the Greek is related to the Hebrew word for compassion, *rachamim*, which refers to the womb of Yahweh. The compassion of Christ comes from such a depth within that it can only be understood as a movement from the very womb of God. When we speak of the compassion of Jesus, we speak of the tenderness and mercy of the infinite, sovereign, almighty God of the universe. When we speak about his ministry, we must grasp that it was far more than a mere hankering for social justice. His care for those around him was birthed from divine urgings found only in the depths of his Father's furious love.

It breaks my heart that I even think to bring this up, but the depravity of man expressed through human trafficking is plain sickening. In almost every continent on the planet, human beings created in the image of God are cheaply trafficked as sex slaves. While people and organizations are rising up against these slave traders, combatting the systemic evil at work, the problem remains: there is a demand for trafficking. Without a craving to buy people for sex, people would not be abducted and sold for sex. This should burn in our guts. Not just because the problem is close to our homes, but because the problem is close to Jesus's heart.

In slowly working through the gospels, we notice Jesus's proficient knack for *seeing* people in need. He had the ability to slow a moment down, no matter how much was going on around him, to look a person in the face; to communicate that they mattered. If we, too, plan on impacting those around us as Christ did, the destitute surrounding us cannot go unseen. No matter how busy our schedules get, no matter how much we attempt to justify our narcissism, the risen Christ beckons us to the ministry of *seeing others*.

We should also keep in mind that because of sin, our compassion leaks. Therefore, if we intend to love as Christ does, it demands we remain in close proximity to our own brokenness. Compassion calls us to frequently remind ourselves of how much grace we have received, otherwise we convince ourselves we have the right to decide who deserves compassion and who gets left out.

Furthermore, *I believe Jesus's ministry changed the world because he set up camp at the intersection of agape and splagchnizomai.* Jesus chose to live and do ministry where love and compassion cross paths, and this is precisely where he calls us to set up camp as well. The love of Christ compels his followers to pitch a tent next to his, smack dab in the middle of love and compassion.

Do For One What You Wish You Could Do For Everyone

At this point, I think it's appropriate to ask questions like: "If my active love does not resemble Christ's, how do I get there? And if I don't have the compassion Christ has for others, how do I get it?" The mystical truth on the matter is we have no control in acquiring this compassion. You want to test it out? Think of the person you despise most on the planet. Now feel for them what Christ does. Like every other human being, you cannot make yourself feel what you don't feel.

One of my favorite songs is Bon Iver's cover of Bonnie Raitt's *I Can't Make You Love Me*. The song beautifully expresses our helplessness to change the human heart: "I can't make you love me if you don't. You can't make your heart feel something it won't. Here in the dark in these final hours, I will lay down my heart and I'll feel the power but you won't."

Sadly, we have no power to change anyone, including ourselves. We have no control over our spiritual formation, and we can do nothing to transform our hearts to Christ's. *The only thing we have control over is whether or not we will surrender our hearts to the One who can change us.* The only authority we carry is an ability to choose whether or not we yield to the work of the Spirit in us. At the end of the day, compassion that moves us from the bowels will simply be a gift of grace. It will be the fruit of our abiding in the vine, and if you remember, *fruit is none of your business.* Our part is abiding well, asking for the gift of compassion, and loving even when we don't feel like loving.

As exemplified in the life and death of Christ, authentic love is hard work. Jesus did not casually go to the cross for us. He was moved with compassion for us, but he still had to make the grueling commitment to love in action, even though he preferred a different method for salvation. Again, we see this articulated in prayer to his Abba in the Garden of Gethsemane, where he essentially asked the Father if they could change plans regarding the cross.[62]

---

62 Luke 22:42

Yet, more than anything else in his life, Jesus was committed to his Father's business, exemplifying for us what it looks like to lay down our will for the Father's: "Not my will, but yours be done."

I turn attention now to an adapted version of a story entitled *The Star Thrower* written by Loren Eiseley.

> "Once upon a time, there was a wise man who used to go to the ocean to do his writing. He had a habit of walking on the beach before he began his work. One day, as he was walking along the shore, he looked down the beach and saw a human figure moving like a dancer. He smiled to himself at the thought of someone who would dance to the day, and so, he walked faster to catch up. As he got closer, he noticed that the figure was that of a young man, and that what he was doing was not dancing at all. The young man was reaching down to the shore, picking up small objects, and throwing them into the ocean. He came closer still and called out 'Good morning! May I ask what it is that you are doing?' The young man paused, looked up, and replied 'Throwing starfish into the ocean.' 'I must ask, then, why are you throwing starfish into the ocean?' asked the somewhat startled wise man. To this, the young man replied, 'The sun is up and the tide is going out. If I don't throw them in, they'll die.' Upon hearing this, the wise man commented, 'But, young man, do you not realize that there are miles and miles of beach and there are starfish all along every mile? You can't possibly make a difference!' At this, the young man bent down, picked up yet another starfish, and threw it into the ocean. As it met the water, he said, 'It made a difference for that one.'"

One of the greatest problems of the Church today may well be that we pray for others too much. I wonder how often we lift people and situations to the Lord in prayer, asking him to bring love, provision, and care to those in need; all the while God wonders why we're doing nothing about it.

We are his body. We are intended to be the expression of his love in the world today. Of course we need to begin with prayer, but if the culmination of our discipleship is praying for others, we will fall short of being the Church Christ intended us to be.

I keep hearing a particular phrase in church circles: "Love God, love people." Recently I heard an even better phrase: "Love God, love people, and do something about it." Sure, the world's desperation for love feels like a weight on our Christian shoulders. At times it appears like unending need, but will we allow this weight to move us to paralysis? We must do something.

As Andy Stanley loves to teach: "Do for one what you wish you could do for everyone." *Do for one person in your life what you wish you could do for thousands.*

I would personally love to provide the homeless masses a place to stay, each abused child, wife, and even husband help in their relationships, and the empty stomachs of our world at least one meal a day. Nevertheless, I admit my limitations while acknowledging my place: I cannot fix the world's problems, but I was not called to either. I may not be able to save the world, but I can reach the one in front of me.

Love considers proximity. If Christians simply committed to loving the person in front of them each moment, the amount of healing and redemption occurring before each sunset would be astounding. We would literally change the world by way of Christ's love. The truth is, though, it really is that simple. Just start throwing starfish, one at a time.

> *"Just as the Father has loved Me,*
> *I have also loved you; abide in My love."*
> *~JOHN 15:9*

Chapter 5
Questions For Personal Reflection and/or
Small Group Discussion

1. Which area do you struggle with most: loving God, loving self, or loving others? What are some practical steps you can take in moving towards the *agape* of Christ in that area?

2. How would the universal Church be seen and thought of if every Christian in the world lived like you and loved others like you?

3. Do you sense a gap between your ability to love externally and your internal love (or compassion for others), especially in regards to people you think should "know better" or are undeserving of that love?

4. What are some practical actions you can do for one, or just a few people, that you wish you could do for many more? And what is preventing you from doing those actions?

CHAPTER 6.1

JOY MADE FULL

-NOT HAPPY-

> *"These things I have spoken to you*
> *so that My joy may be in you,*
> *and that your joy may be made full."*
> ~JOHN 15:11

> *"God, you have made us for yourself,*
> *and our hearts are ever restless until they rest in you."*
> ST. AUGUSTINE OF HIPPO

Joy Beyond Happiness

We're addicted to results. We strive for years in hopes of attaining the deepest desires of our hearts, but we soon find ourselves with an empty effort tank, and stuck in a satisfaction famine. Our goals are left wanting. A position, a career, a home, getting married, having children, making enough money to feel secure... We may in time, finally achieve our dream, but then we discover we actually haven't. We're less fulfilled than ever, and even more conscious of the numbness of our hearts.

Where did we go wrong? And maybe just as important a question: where do we go from here? I recommend turning once again to Jesus's statement found in verse eleven: "These things I have spoken to you so that My joy may be in you, and that your joy may be made full."

Two important elements of this verse immediately rise to the surface:

1) Jesus wants his followers to be joyful people;
2) and their joy is not yet full.

But why does Jesus speak the wonders of the first ten verses just for joy? And what is it about *his* joy that makes the previous content culminate in it? Brennan Manning argued that the living presence of Jesus awakened joy and set people free; that joy was in fact the most characteristic result of all Jesus's ministry to ragamuffins.

Because Jesus intentionally speaks about joy, we should distinguish it from happiness. I assume if you ask 100 people what they want in life, you'll receive a similar answer from many: "I want to be happy." The problem with happiness, though, is that we can't grab onto it for long periods of time. We attempt to look ahead past our difficulties to the day or season we'll finally chain down happiness for good, but it seems to set itself free over and over again.

In the 2015 commencement speech at the University of Houston, Matthew McConaughey articulated his thoughts on happiness and joy.

"Happiness is an emotional response to an outcome—If I win I will be happy, if I don't I won't. An if-then, cause and effect, quid pro quo standard that we cannot sustain because we immediately raise it every time we attain it. You see, happiness demands a certain outcome; it is result reliant. If happiness is what you're after, then you are going to be let down frequently and be unhappy much of your time. Joy, though, is something else. It's not a choice, not a response to some result, it is a constant. Joy is the feeling we have from doing what we are fashioned to do, no matter the outcome."

I agree with McConaughey. Happiness in life is outwardly focused, dependent on circumstances, situations, people, and emotions. It is fleeting, transient, and inconsistent. Consequently, the disappointment we experience from chasing happiness is due to the fact that inner peace has little to do with external outcomes. But we are oh so easily seduced by hallucinations of a permanent happiness.

Much like the law of diminishing returns, those things we achieve leave us unfulfilled and continuously in want. We grasp for happiness, but the goal, nevertheless, remains elusive. A forever-happiness continues to collapse before us because it no more exists than a leprechaun promising it. And while multitudes trek tenaciously after what they believe to be the pursuit of happiness, their search is, in reality, a quest for joy.

Joy, unlike happiness, can be seen as a holy contentment. Dallas Willard described joy as, "Our portion in Christ's fellowship... robust with no small element of outright hilarity in it."[63] It is a satisfied peace in the acknowledgment that we are not in charge of anything. Joy, in contrast to happiness, offers an inner serenity beyond external conditions or emotional positions. By its nature, joy bears witness at our gut level, allowing it to remain despite changing surroundings. In short, happiness searches for peace in how things are going. Joy finds peace in the person of Jesus.

---

63 Dallas Willard, *The Divine Conspiracy: Rediscovering Our Hidden Life In God*, 290-291.

Moreover, what makes joy so powerful is its cyclical nature: when we enter into the agape of Christ- a *love* beyond feelings- we're ushered into the joy of Christ- a *contentment* beyond feelings. Christ's joy, then, drives us back into his love, once again creating in us capacity for more joy at a depth we could not handle before.

While it may be easy agreeing with the beginning paragraphs of this chapter, why is it that many Christians make for miserable company? Why is it that Christians are some of the worst partiers on the planet? Richard Foster claims, "Holy joy is one of the most common marks of those whole in the power of the Spirit."[64] We should be the most joyful people in town- no exaggeration. We should be the best party-throwers in our neighborhoods.

The world is in dire need of more joyful Christians. The message of our lives should communicate that following Jesus is not a depressing experience, but a euphoric excursion in the Spirit. According to Jesus, discipleship to him leads to pure joy. However, if this is truly the case, why the schism between the full joy about which Jesus speaks, and the emptiness in the hearts of many who call him Lord?

I think I've come up with a decent method for identifying at a basic level if we're joyful people or not. Here's a quick and simple test. Just answer honestly. How easily frustrated are you by being inconvenienced? How upset do you find yourself when things don't go for you as planned, or if your intentions are thwarted? In general, joyful people have less trouble with this than do happy people.

Maybe you're reading this thinking: "I'm a Christian. I live my life for Christ, for the most part, but I wouldn't consider myself miserable company. I just don't live in that 'contented peace beyond circumstances' you're talking about." A lot of Christians would likely label themselves happy people but not joyful people;

---

64 Richard Foster, *Streams of Living Water: Essential Practices from the Six Great Traditions of Christian Faith*, 104.

not necessarily mean or angry individuals, simply that stress and anxiety seem to consistently weasel into the fabric of their lives.

I meet with Christians regularly who are quite familiar with the words of Jesus in Matthew 11: "Come to Me, all who are weary and heavy-laden, and I will give you rest. Take My yoke upon you and learn from Me, for I am gentle and humble in heart, and you will find rest for your souls. For My yoke is easy and My burden is light." Yet, life seems to continually get the best of them. While they dream for Jesus's new life invitation to be true for them, stress, anxiety, and worry just seem to be all too familiar in their heads and hearts on a daily basis. Joy remains constantly unattainable.

Three Factors Robbing Christians Of Joy

Not to claim there are only three factors at play, but in my ministry experience I've recognized a few patterns echoing in the stories of those with whom I've journeyed.

1) Clinical Depression: Firstly, depression in the life of a Christian is entirely possible. This may not be a struggle for all Christians, but it is a reality for some.

I've heard that clinical depression affects almost 19 million adults every year. It's a sickness, so it aggravates me to overhear a Christian tell someone with depression they just need to pray more and move on. True, our culture may flippantly throw the word around more than necessary, but clinical depression is far worse than a lingering sadness. It severely interferes with a person's daily functioning.

For many, depression is an issue of biology and chemistry, not just emotion. Clinical depression is triggered by an imbalance of several chemicals in the brain, and is treated by an appropriate prescription for antidepressants. Expecting someone clinically depressed to stop being lazy or self-pitying is no less ridiculous than expecting a diabetic needing daily insulin shots to merely eat differently and move on. So although true joy is a result of the abiding life, Christians get sick, and depression is a sickness. Joy in the life of an abiding Christian may in fact be partnered with the wonderful gift of modern medicine.

If you think you may struggle with clinical depression, don't let your pride get in the way. Go get it checked out. There's no shame in meeting with a professional to explore whether or not you're in need of medication; and there should be no shame in taking that medication if it is prescribed. There are people I greatly respect who take anti-depressants in order to balance out their brain chemistry. Depression is real, so we need to deal with it appropriately.

2) Perspective: Perspective tends to be a weighty factor here as well. Having full joy does not mean life will be easy. Jesus told his followers that discipleship to him would be no simple task. In fact, discipleship to Jesus is far from a mere coping mechanism to get us *through life*; it is the entrance through which we are offered completely *new life*. Therefore, we need to learn to shift our perspective in the midst of difficulty.

I have a dear friend who's an avid runner. In conversation with her one day she explained a shift in her perspective regarding approaching hills. Here is what she communicated to me:

> "I used to have a lot of anxiety about running hills. What didn't work for me was trying to conquer the hills by charging at them full force. That approach might work for short hills on short runs, but it was of no use on long runs where the inclines were sometimes several miles long and I still had hours left and more upcoming hills on the route.
>
> A marathon-training book I read had a much better approach. So much of distance running is mental, and that's the area that needs the most training. Instead of seeing hills as the enemy or even a challenge, greet each hill with, 'Well, hello there, hill. Come run with me' or, 'Let's

run together for awhile.' It seems cheesy, but it's about a deeper paradigm shift. The hills are no longer obstacles, they're companions.

When my perspective shifts, the anxiety goes away and my legs and lungs are able to relax. When I see hills as the enemy, I'm always dreading them. They consume my thoughts before the run and actually diminish my performance. When I see them as my companion, I work with them instead of against them. It doesn't matter if the hill is small or a monster climb... the harder the hill, the 'more' of a companion I have for that section of the run."

Contrary to what the "spiritual warfare expert" at your church may have told you, rough times are not always sent from the devil to destroy you. In line with the thoughts of James and Paul, difficulties can actually be thought of as our companions for the journey in equipping us with capacity for full joy. On one hand, we should not belittle that we are in spiritual war with an enemy who hates us, but demons are not hiding behind every trashcan. The annoying and/or mean people in your life are not marionettes from *Hades*. They may in fact be Godsends and companions to be worked *with* rather than *against*.

I encourage you to welcome a shift in perspective. Embrace the inconvenience. *We don't learn joy by getting what we want; we often learn it by getting what we don't want.* Sure, life may draw us into the heart of darkness, but joy recognizes there is no dark place God is not greater than. Therefore, when you face opposition, difficulty, and/or conflict, lean into it rather than run from it. The Lord would love to use it to strengthen you and create more space in you to carry the joy you were designed to hold.

Teresa of Avila wrote substantial work on the consolations of God- the deep, felt presence of God in and with us that consoles and comforts us through life. Concerning our prayer lives, she claimed: "Joyful consolations in prayer have their beginning in our own human nature and end in God. True joy however begins in God and human nature is allowed to feel and enjoy them. Praying for consolations do not expand the heart; rather they usually seem to constrain it a little."[65] Essentially what she's communicating is to stop praying for God to make your load lighter, and start praying for legs strong enough to carry what he's asked of you for this season. Perspective.

3) The Triangle: Finally, when I hear people venting about how stressed out they are from all the conspiring elements of their lives, my mind immediately goes to "the Triangle." I referenced the Triangle in chapter 2.2 if you'd like to refer back to it. The conclusion I've come to is that virtually every expanse of stress and anxiety in our lives will find its root in at least one area, if not a combination of the three areas from the Triangle.

To remind you again, the three regions of the Triangle are: the desire to influence the actions of others, the desire to influence how circumstances will turn out, and the desire to influence how people think and feel about us. The Triangle battles in our subconscious for us to take control of life, convincing us to believe if we can make people do what we want them to, make situations turn out how we want them to, and make people feel and think of us the way we want them to, we will be happy.

Remember, though, happiness is short-lived, and just about the time we're settling into it, it's on its way out. Why? *Because circumstances are constantly changing.* People change how they act, situations flip upside down, and people change their view about others consistently. If you simply focus on influencing these outward components, the chase for control over the Triangle will loiter until it drives you mad.

Our aim should be centered on handing over the results of the Triangle to the One who actually has the ability to influence it. In

---

65 Teresa of Avila, *The Collected Works of St. Teresa of Avila: Volume 2- The Way of Perfection, Meditation on the Song of Songs, and The Interior Castle*, 318.

doing so, we set ourselves up to receive the full joy of Christ that is not reliant on any circumstances. This doesn't mean we won't get upset, hurt, or sad. Even Jesus got frustrated. We're human beings built to experience emotion, which is extremely healthy for our souls. We can, in fact, experience sadness, anger, sorrow, and grief, while maintaining a sense of holy contentment, but we must learn to release the results of the Triangle if we hope to have a chance at joy beyond conditional happiness.

Ultimately, if we hope to be joyful people, we have to give way for existence beyond happiness. Full joy may include happiness, but it is not limited to it. And what you'll find is happiness doesn't satisfy like joy does. Joy is a fuel that burns hotter and brighter and longer than happiness ever could. It quenches the soul's thirst to a level that, in comparison, makes happiness taste like saltwater.

Jesus truly longs to give us this joy, but we continue to figure out new and creative ways to deny this magnificent gift. Receiving takes our participation, and that's what the next chapter is aimed at.

CHAPTER 6.2

Joy Made Full
-THIS JOY IS MINE-

> *"These things I have spoken to you*
> *so that My joy may be in you,*
> *and that your joy may be made full."*
> ~John 15:11

> *"God, you have made us for yourself,*
> *and our hearts are ever restless until they rest in you."*
> St. Augustine of Hippo

Receiving This Joy

I f Jesus wants this joy for our lives, and we're currently not experiencing it, Captain Obvious might curiously ask, "How, then, does one receive this joy?" Please note, in no way am I attempting to provide a comprehensive list for achieving joy, nor should a person follow the suggestions below like steps on a ladder to obtaining some level of spiritual enlightenment. However, if you find yourself struggling to live in the joy of the Spirit, I simply recommend trying out some of the following ideas. If you can begin to practice even some of these on a daily basis, I believe soon enough, with the help of the Holy Spirit, you will be able to claim with confidence, "This joy is mine."

Shift *your motivation from achieving the joy of Christ, to adamantly abiding in Christ.* I believe less in the pursuit of happiness than I do in the happiness of pursuit. Ironically, as we chase happiness it continues to elude us. The truth of happiness is that it allows itself to be experienced only as a *byproduct* of being fully immersed in a moment. And it only lasts for that moment.

The secret to joy, however, is quite simple: joy comes by virtue of committing to abide in the vine. We must realize that joy, pure joy, full joy is a gift of grace to us. It will not be experienced due to our stubborn grasping at it. It tenderly makes its way into our hearts by way of disciplined abiding. Joy is the natural result, the fruit, of the abiding life. Very likely, if we're not experiencing the joy for which we were built, we are not abiding with the fortitude for which we were built.

I think to how American culture so blatantly influences our desires for an "attractive" body. The truth is, however, you can wish and pray all you want for the body you want, but without altering your eating habits, your sleep schedule, or the regularity of your workouts, you will never have that body. Similarly, you can try as hard as you want to attain joy, but unless you commit to the actions that in fact produce joy- abiding in the vine- joy will remain an impossible reality.

My favorite TV show of all time is LOST. There's an inspiring scene between two main characters in the show, John Locke and Sun, in which this conversation develops:

Sun: "I don't think I've ever seen you angry."
Locke: "Oh, I used to get angry- all the time; frustrated too."
Sun: "You're not frustrated any more?"
Locke: "I'm not lost any more."
Sun: "How did you do that?"
Locke: "The same way anything lost gets found- I stopped looking."

Eugene Peterson's approach to this topic proves beneficial here: "Joy is not a requirement of Christian discipleship, it is a consequence…Joy is what God gives, not what we work up."[66] Essentially what I'm getting at is, stop chasing after joy. Shift your focus to abiding well; joy naturally follows.

This first recommendation admits that ultimately, we receive the multilayered grace of God because he wants to give it; it is his acting and our receiving. However, while joy reveals itself as a gracious gift from God, we can also choose to participate with God's grace. Accordingly, besides abiding well, there are things we can do to set ourselves up to receive joy.

Choose your relationships wisely. I remember an illustration shown to me once by a friend. He had me stand on a chair and asked me to pull him up to where I was. I tried, and failed. Then he yanked my hand and I fell off quickly. He told me that although I am called to live missionally in this world and love people well, it is much easier to pull someone down than up.

In that light, hang with joyful people. Surround yourself with individuals who are annoyingly joyful at times. Build intentional relationships with those who exemplify the joy Christ speaks of. Joy can be rather contagious.

Determine to be thankful for the life God has given you. Again, this is about perspective. Is your glass of water half full or half empty? Who cares?! You have a glass of water! Resolve to maintain a thankful heart no matter your circumstances, and focus on your blessings rather than emptiness or places of lack.

If you're reading this book, you can be thankful you have enough of an education to do so. If you bought this book, you can be thankful you had the money to buy it. If someone bought it for you or is allowing you to borrow it, you can be thankful for a friend who cares about you. And I'm hoping you didn't steal the book…

---

66 Eugene H. Peterson, *A Long Obedience in the Same Direction: Discipleship in an Instant Society*, 96, 100.

We swiftly move from gratitude to expectation to entitlement. In all truth, your life could be much worse. Maybe you need to take a few minutes and literally write out a list of things you can choose to be thankful for. A meal today, a close friend, a roof to sleep under, clothes for the day, transportation, a pet, even the physical strength to remain breathing.

I encourage you to kick yourself in the butt, stop complaining about what you think you lack, and decide to be a soul radically defined by gratitude and appreciation. Whether or not you've realized or admitted it yet, God has been exceptionally good to you.

Resist *the temptation to compare your life against those around you.* I think back to my first time at Kipu Falls in Kauai. Per the suggestion of a "Kauai Secrets Book," we parked our car next to a particular sugar cane field, walked through the cane for a good five minutes, and eventually wound up at this beautiful waterfall that seemed to come out of nowhere.

I ran to the top and looked down at the 25-foot drop. People were swimming below; others were jumping off the rocks atop the waterfall. I mustered up the courage and was about to jump when the guy next to me turned around, smiled at me, and did a huge backflip into the water below. I thought to myself, "There's no way I'm going to do a back flip off this thing." But as I compared myself against the guy who jumped off the rock cooler than I would, I considered not jumping at all. "My jump will look lame if I go after this guy."

Eventually I convinced myself it would be stupid not to jump just because someone else could do it with more grace. So I jumped. Yes, it probably looked like I was being maliciously tickled all the way down, but I jumped. And I jumped again, and again. The joy I experienced that day was in direct relation to my decision not to compare myself to another.

Regrettably, in fear of how they will be thought of by another, or even thought of by themselves, people are failing to jump into

the greatness that could be their lives, thereby missing the joy waiting for them. Don't allow fear by comparison to be the motivating
force behind your decision-making. It will rob you of the abundant
joy waiting for you in Christ.

Read *of those in Scripture who joyed in suffering.* In reality, most
of us have never truly suffered. Most of us have not received real
persecution because of our faith. We read James 1: "Consider it
joy when you go through trials…" and we attempt to put a smile
on our faces when our cars break down or the jerk at work keeps
embarrassing us. But take a moment to reflect on the persecution of someone like the apostle Paul: he was beaten, shackled,
whipped, mocked, shipwrecked, imprisoned, stoned, and eventually murdered for his faith. Not only did Paul have a significantly
more difficult life than the great majority of us, he was harassed for
his faith in Christ. YET, how did he respond? What was the posture of Paul's heart in response to the difficulties and treatment he
regularly received? His declaration: "Therefore I am well content
with weaknesses, with insults, with distresses, with persecutions,
with difficulties, for Christ's sake; for when I am weak, then I am
strong."[67] *Well content*! Paul clung to a holy satisfaction in everything he suffered because each trial, each tribulation, each persecution brought him back to his knees before Jesus.

Many wonder why amazing miracle stories happen in other
countries around the globe, while we don't see as much of the su-
pernatural in our own lives. The answer could simply be that we
don't think we need God much.

To use an example: let's say later tonight you get a headache.
Is your first thought to get on your knees and ask for healing, or
to walk over to the pantry and find some ibuprofen? By no means
am I lumping all Christians into this group, but between our pay-
checks and quick access to things like food, water, medicine, and
clothes, we've become accustomed to life without God. A great

---

67 2 Corinthians 12:10

number of people in the world are lucky to have one meal a day, are dying of diseases, are living in poverty, and realize that without the grace and help of God today, they are literally dead tomorrow.

God has made us to need him, and we keep finding ways not to. Leaning into difficult circumstances, choosing to be well content in them, even thanking God for them fosters in us a protection from the obsession of self-reliance. Looking to those in Scripture who went through terrible trials and persecutions, even to death, and seeing how they responded can be an encouragement to us. It puts into perspective how blessed we are and how much the Lord wants to use our circumstances for his glory.

Allow the family of God in Scripture to be for you what they are: heroes, giants, and exemplars of our faith on whose shoulders we stand to embrace the love of Christ.

Sabbath well. Work hard, play hard. You need to know when to stop, and you need to know how you, personally, need to stop. Sabbath is a gift from the Lord, but it is a gift only enjoyed by those who take time to unwrap its layers.

I know, it's difficult to convince ourselves we need, or even have the time, to take a day off work. We feel such pressure to move quickly into the next week by striving another day into existence. The world's standards, rationality, and economy of time plea desperately to fill up our calendars, manipulating us to think we can accomplish more today and enjoy its rewards tomorrow. But sadly, we won't actually allow ourselves to enjoy tomorrow when it gets here, for tomorrow will gently draw us into the work needing to be done for tomorrow's tomorrow. The economy of time God protects, on the other hand, is an entirely different world. Here, Sabbath is never a waste. It brings restoration and wholeness to a soul more in need of rest than it even realizes.

There's a saying: "We have all the time we need to do the things God has asked of us." When we work hard for the Lord, we should no doubt lay our heads to rest at night tired, but we should only feel burnt out when we entertain work outside God's permission.

We are drawn, *by fruit*, to work outside the realm of what God has asked of us. But if you recall, fruit is none of our business. When we're not concerned about fruit, about the Triangle, we can rest well. When we place boundaries around the stuff in our lives, the people in our lives, and the problems in our lives, a beautiful stillness appears; a stillness enabling us to find the joy already lodged deep in our souls, dependent on nothing external for existence. Here in this unique territory, Sabbath becomes a joy rather than a burden.

I love the water basin illustration. Imagine holding a basin of water. As you shake the basin, the water swishes from side to side. But as you still your hands and look to the calming surface, your reflection begins to reveal itself. The less you move, the more accurately you see yourself. Here we discover one of the wonders of Sabbath: as you move less, literally and figuratively, not only do you gain strength, but you also begin to see a truer reflection of your own soul.

I do realize for some of you, a whole day of rest is impossible. A single mom with three kids and two jobs would likely argue this point well. It does not, however, invalidate your necessity for rest. Be intentional about finding little Sabbaths throughout your day to enjoy. Before heading off to work in the morning, stop for a moment to breathe in the sunrise. When sitting at a stoplight, close your eyes for twenty seconds and clear your mind. Before bed, slip outside and enjoy the stars for a few minutes. Allow yourself to be enraptured by the splendor of a savory cup of coffee.

Sabbath is not about a day; it's about a mindset. It helps us accept that we need rest before we think we need rest; that we need to stop before we think we need to stop; that our work should actually birth out of our rest rather than the opposite. And it tells

God we believe he can accomplish more in our stopping than we can in our striving.

As an example, one of my favorite ways to Sabbath is watching film. I usually end up watching a couple films each week. These two-four hours are invaluable to me. I don't have to think about work, relationships, bills, church, or even God- sorry if that offends you... My mind gets a short break to get lost in the power of story, and it's often enough to rejuvenate me for what lies ahead. This is by no means my only time of Sabbath, but it is a vital one for me.

It would do you well to find a few activities you can participate in for short periods of time that will give you a "checkout." Maybe gardening, listening to music, making specialty coffee, going for a run, water coloring, stargazing, hiking, reading the comics, or working out. Find some activities that don't require much work or thinking from you that you can enjoy consistently. You need rest before you think you need rest, if only because your joy may be waiting for you to stop and breathe.

Talk to yourself rather than listen to yourself. We all have an inner voice that likes to vent. It's an inner dialogue that when left to its own, will usually lead us down a path of complaining, sorrow, and comparison.

The goal here is to shift from being a passive listener in your inner dialogue, to an active catalyst for your thought life. The next time something goes wrong, rather than complain in your head or compare your life up against someone who has it better than you, talk to yourself about how blessed you are. Lead yourself down a road of confidence and hope in God. Inform yourself of how far you've come and next steps to take. Joy for you may be sitting just beyond leading yourself.

Ask God for joy. One of my mantras in life is, "Why not ask?" To illustrate, one night I hung out with some friends for a few hours at Downtown Disney. As I was leaving the parking lot, the man at the toll both asked me for my ticket. I gave it to him and he told me I owed $7. I thought to myself: "Why not ask?" So I asked the man: "Any chance my parking can be free tonight?" He replied, "Why would I do that?" I said with a smile on my face, "Because you're a nice guy." He paused for a moment. Then he asked me what I do. I told him I was a pastor in Hawthorne. He responded, "Hey, my parents live close to you. Have a nice night." And the gate opened. I drove away thinking: that's exactly why I ask!

The point behind my mantra is this: if I did not ask, I would have paid $7; if I did ask and he said no, I would have paid $7; but there was a chance that in asking, he would let me go for free, and there is no way I would go free unless I asked. Henceforth, "Why not ask?"

Funny enough, I actually ask for a ton of free stuff regularly. Food, coffee beans and brewing equipment, books, upgrades in hotels, all kinds of experiences... You name it. I don't really mind someone declining my request, so I get turned down frequently, but I also get some cool stuff every so often.

I think to some extent, this mantra translates into our walks with God as well. Why not ask for his pure joy? If you don't ask, you may not get it. You could ask for it and he may not give it to you. Or you could ask for pure joy and have the possibility of receiving it because our God loves to give gifts to his kids.

In the words of Teresa of Avila: "God's joy is not a joy the intellect obtains merely through desire. It is enkindled without understanding how. It is simply a gift from the Lord, who gives according to who he is, not who we are."[68] In small ways, joy is a quality of the abiding life we participate in receiving, but it is predominantly a gift from God; a demonstration of the extreme benevolence of our loving Father who lavishes grace on his kids. So ask for it.

---

68 Teresa of Avila. *The Collected Works of St. Teresa of Avila: Volume 2- The Way of Perfection, Meditation on the Song of Songs, and The Interior Castle*, 131.

Freedom in Joy

Once more, I want to come back to the idea of fruit. Fruit is results, outcomes, and future consequences to past or present moment decisions- and it is none of your business. Your business is adequately being with God and abiding in him, in order that your will might be aligned with his; then you set your heart on obedience.

Now, usually God doesn't provide step-by-step, minute-by-minute instructions for how we're to go about our lives. He may simply point us in the right direction and ask us to figure it out as we go. Thus, abiding doesn't necessarily produce a certainty about where to go or what actions come next, but it will create a commitment to obedience before we even know what God asks of us- *committing to the "what" before we know the "how"*.

Additionally, the extent to which you are fruit minded will determine the extent to which you will stress on this side of heaven. On the other hand, your ability to surrender outcomes to Jesus will create in you the ability to bear joy. When we're fruit minded, we're often trying to figure out solutions to problems Jesus isn't trying to fix at the moment. If you can discipline yourself to focus your attention and intention on what he is up to in your life, you will end up using your energy purely on things he's focused on. Here, in this posture of the heart, we find our stress diminished and our joy catalyzed.

This approach to life also gracefully breaks down the wall between sacred and secular. We don't have to attempt finding joy in the "things of God" while suffering through or distancing ourselves from "things outside of God." Excluding sin, everything we do is in God. We can live every moment in pure joy because our Savior has brought life to our life.

A.W. Tozer wrote, "It is not what a man does that determines whether his work is sacred or secular, it is why he does it. The motive is everything."[69] Grocery shopping, tying your shoes, sit-

---

69 A.W. Tozer, *The Pursuit of God*, 127.

ting in traffic, reading a book about miniature schnauzers, eating strawberries, weighing out coffee beans... No second is wasted with Jesus. Every moment is an opportunity to live out the full joy made available to you through a life of abiding. Every moment can be made holy because of the intent of our hearts.

To a couple happily married for fifty years, joy with each other is no longer contingent upon the activities they experience together. Although they may enjoy reading together, swimming, or walking to the park for a picnic, joy resides in the depth of their love and covenant union.

This joy-producing love testifies to the greatness of our God, and it juxtaposes itself against the happiness the world attempts to produce in us. Basically, what I think Jesus was communicating to his disciples in John 15 is this: "The world will look at the joy I've given you and they won't know what to make of it, but something in their gut will want it too because they'll know you're freer than they are."

His joy is freedom from the world's games. It's freedom from the world's seductive pleasures. When we receive the full joy of Christ, we find that the Spirit protects it at such a depth within us the world can't touch it. Or as Albert Camus powerfully wrote: "The only way to deal with an un-free world is to become so absolutely free that your very act of existence is an act of rebellion."[70] Life in Christ is indeed rebellion by joy.

Subtle Self-Righteousness

At some point in our lives, maybe even currently, every one of us has had a sin or lifestyle we couldn't seem to shake. You want to serve Christ as he asks; you want to live in obedience to him, but that sin or lifestyle continues to incessantly seduce you, making

---

70 Albert Camus, referenced by Brennan Manning in *The Signature of Jesus: A Path to Living a Life of Holy Passion and Unreasonable Faith*, 79.

you feel powerless. Your Christian life, in many ways, ends up being about outlasting temptation; just not sinning.

When you've not sinned for a while, you feel on top of the world, and your relationship with Christ is more beautiful than it has ever been. And the day you slip up, you feel like you wandered miles from the path you were on. Much like the signs you find at a construction yard or metal shop that claim, "Accident free for _____ days," life in Christ can center around the clock. "Just avoid sinning for as long as you can, and when you mess up, the clock gets reset."

This approach to following Jesus reminds me of the "Red Queen Principle," referring to a conversation between Alice and the Red Queen in Lewis Carroll's *Through The Looking-Glass*. At a certain point in the tale, Alice discovers she must run fast only to remain in the same spot. She asserts that in her country, one would generally get somewhere else if he or she ran very fast for a long time. The Queen replies that in her land, it takes all the running one can do to remain in the same place.

Like Alice, we may end up running tirelessly in our faith journey, only to remain in the same place. The problem with this kind of thinking, though, is that the clock becomes our aim rather than God. Our entire Christian life at this point centers on sin management rather than intimacy with Christ. And while it seems like our motives are right, we end up believing we have the ability to figure out how to live Christ-like in our own power; a form of self-righteousness. *But life change is not something you do; it is something that is done to you by yielding to the work of the Spirit in you.* Righteousness is not attainable; it's offered.

I think back to the story I told at the beginning of the book about the little girl and her mother in the canoe. To remind you, the mother was in the back with an oar, rowing for direction. The young daughter sat in the front, arbitrarily slapping her paddle at the water. More than half the time this little girl was flicking water forward and sideways, making it more difficult for the mother to point the canoe in the right direction. The girl, intently striving to move the canoe, thought her paddling was making significant impacts on where the canoe was headed. In reality, her paddling was hurting the overall direction. But the mother seemed completely content with her daughter. If I had to guess, the mother's focus was not necessarily on where they were headed, but on the fact that they were in the boat together.

Taking a different approach to this story than I did at the beginning of the book, I think the Lord is less concerned with our performance, even less concerned with the direction of our lives, as he is with us committing to being in the boat with him. You see, the point of all this is not that we finally figure out the abiding life. *The point of all this is intimacy with Christ- which actually is finally figuring out the abiding life.* We put undue pressure on ourselves by trying as hard as we do to live virtuously, embracing our own self-righteous tendencies, while God is more concerned with the posture of our hearts. Rather than right actions, he desires right hearts. And with hearts set on surrender to Jesus, in due time, sin will work its way out.

M. Basil Pennington put it this way: "I have run into a situation in marriage counseling a number of times. The couple is unhappy. The wife is dissatisfied and the husband cannot see why. He goes into a long recital of all he is doing for her. He is holding down two or three jobs, building a new house, buying her everything. But to all this the wife quietly replies: If only he would stop for a few minutes and give me himself!"[71] I imagine God at times, as he looks upon us hurrying about in all our (self) righteous activities, saying to himself: "If only they would stop for a few minutes and give me themselves."

As I recall and reflect on the countless conversations I've shared with friends over many cups of coffee, I cannot help but

71 M. Basil Pennington, *Daily We Touch Him*, 51-52.

see patterns. Meetings back-to-back-to-back, sifting through the murky, confusing, painful situations of life. Friends yearning for contentment, doing everything they think necessary to attain contentment, all the while, missing the only thing actually necessary for contentment.

A friend of mine says I'm formulaic without being legalistic. I'll wear my formula badge for a moment. I see a simple formula for contentment. It goes like this: *intimacy leads to trust, which leads to contentment.*

Here's the explanation. True contentment in life on this side of eternity, full joy, is only possible due to a radical trust in the person of Jesus. Basically, we can get to the point where we peacefully accept everything happening to or around us in life because we trust that Jesus is in charge; where we actually believe Psalm 23:1- The Lord is our shepherd, and we lack nothing. We come to believe we are better off in his hands than we are in our own. Therefore, while we still have the ability to experience healthy, yet uncomfortable emotions, what remains is an enduring sense of peace because we know in our guts Jesus is in charge. However, the only way we will ever develop this kind of trust in Jesus is through intimacy with him. How do we build trust in anyone? Through time spent together, allowing them to prove themselves faithful and trustworthy. In time, intimacy births trust naturally, and trust births contentment naturally. You want contentment? Avoid chasing it. Go after intimacy.

I remember sitting with God once, in the quiet alone. I asked him to give me something to pray, something he would pray through me. Here's what came out: *"Jesus, help me to be content in everything, but satisfied in nothing but you."* I want to be able to experience any moment in life, delightful or dreadful, and have my contentment protected in the depths of my soul; but ultimately, I want everything in life to leave me unsatisfied. My marriage, my family, my job, my hobbies, my passions, my possessions... I want all of it to leave me thirsty before Jesus. I want Jesus to be the only thing that satisfies my soul. And I have not stopped praying this prayer.

Herein lies the beauty of John 15: Abiding in Christ leads us to a loving union with him that produces full joy in us. Joy becomes the natural overflow of one's intimacy with God, bursting into every facet of our lives.

To further clarify: joy comes simply from abiding in the true vine. Joy becomes our reality as we realize, with the help of grace, that we are fully known, fully loved, and fully accepted by Jesus just as we are. Eventually peace beyond circumstance is effortless because it has been done to us.

Rather than chasing after joy, aim your efforts at chasing after Jesus. *The pursuit of Jesus is the only effective approach to receiving the full joy he offers.*

Finally, I echo over you the concluding prayer in the book of Jude: "Now to Him who is able to keep you from stumbling, and to make you stand in the presence of His glory blameless with great joy, to the only God our Savior, through Jesus Christ our Lord, be glory, majesty, dominion and authority, before all time and now and forever. Amen."[72]

> *"These things I have spoken to you*
> *so that My joy may be in you,*
> *and that your joy may be made full."*
> **~JOHN 15:11**

---

72 Jude 1:24-25

Chapter 6
Questions For Personal Reflection and/or
Small Group Discussion

1. Happiness is externally based; joy exists beyond circumstances. Would you, then, consider yourself a joyful soul, a happy soul, or neither?

2. Have your prayers been more about God lightening your load rather than giving you strength to carry what he's asked of you? What are some things he has asked you to carry for this season?

3. Are you lacking joy because you're still focused on controlling the Triangle- influencing people to do what you want them to/ influencing situations to turn out how you want them to/ influencing people to think or feel about you how you want them to?

4. Do you Sabbath regularly? If so, how? If not, what are some ways you can find small periods of time to stop and breathe regularly?

5. Have you been chasing joy more than abiding in Christ?

A WORD AFTER

Rudyard Kipling once said, "I am, by calling, a dealer in words; and words are, of course, the most powerful drug used by mankind." As a pastor, I can completely relate. My job demands caring for people, frequently through words. It requires discerning which words to communicate in the right time, and whether or not a situation needs words at all. And while Kipling's statement carries a potent truth, I prefer to take it a step further.

I too, am a dealer in words, but only God has the power to take words and lodge them in a soul's alcoves. Any beautifully constructed sentence or well-crafted phrase will eventually wither. If anything substantial is to take root, blame must be passed to the awe-inspiring work of the Spirit planting it.

Furthermore, my desire for this book is that the words on the pages before you would not simply act as inked paper to fill time, or even an intoxicating drug; but rather, that your heart would be softened to the work of the Spirit in you through reading and reflecting over your place in the narrative of God's love.

I would like to resolve this book with three concluding thoughts. The first is in light of Brother Lawrence's *The Practice of the Presence of God*. If you've never read the book, please go read it after you finish this one. It's easily in my top five favorite books. And while it is a short read, it is life changing nonetheless.

Brother Lawrence served as a lay brother in a Carmelite monastery in 17th century Paris. In this book compiled after his death, Brother Lawrence claimed God drew him to such a level of intimacy that he believed there to be no difference between his time washing dishes or repairing sandals, and his time in prayer, worship, or reading Scripture. His whole life was holy worship; life lived unto God. The book, which is actually a collection of letters and conversations with Brother Lawrence, inspires readers to seek Christ continuously throughout the day.

Brother Lawrence's life message was simple: *think about God as often as you can, in all you do, and pray for help to do it more.* Astonishingly, he stated that the last forty years of his life were experienced in moment by moment practicing the presence of God; forty years of a quiet familiar conversation with Jesus, is how he described it.

Speaking personally, an hour is challenging for me, but I have committed to grow in practicing the presence of God. I have committed to thinking of God more throughout my day, which breaks down the distinction that my "time with Jesus" is holier than walking my dog, responding to emails, or kicking around a soccer ball with my daughter. The Lord is present to me always; why should I not be present to him always?

This concept also empowers us to live out what Paul advised in Romans 12. Whether you think it to be true or not, you have the ability to offer everything you are to God in worship. Not just your prayers, reading your Bible, singing songs to him, or giving tithes to him; but offering all of life as worship unto him.

Brother Lawrence's encouragement to his friends was to never leave God alone. Practicing the presence of God is a purposeful entry into a deepened awareness of the presence and action of God in the life of a Christian.

I bring this up because I believe there to be no better way of abiding than practicing the presence. Thomas Merton contended, "People who only know how to think about God during fixed periods of the day will never get very far in the spiritual life. In fact, they will not even think of Him in the moments they have religiously marked for mental prayer."[73]

There is no holy location or time. Jesus offers the privilege of abiding in him all day. If you want to train yourself in becoming a more disciplined abider, try abiding more throughout your day, bringing to memory the presence and action of God in your life whenever you can and wherever you go.

Oddly, many of us have learned to pray that God would be with us during the day, but his presence with us is a given. What's in question is whether or not we will choose to be with him during the day. If we thought of Jesus more throughout our day, do you think we would represent him more accurately? Do you think we would be more obedient to him? Try it out.

Secondly, I want to bring your attention back to the notion that fruit is none of your business. While I hope you're beginning to sift through how this principle can be applied in your own life, I figured I would communicate one more example in which I am personally and currently practicing it.

Again, fruit is results, outcomes, and consequences to present moment decisions. I think now to all the fruit of what this book could potentially produce. This book could change lives, or everyone who reads it could literally set it on fire with disgust. It could sell 10,000 copies, or it could end up being a sympathy-read by my friends and family because no one is interested enough to even finish the first chapter. Its profits could bring me extreme wealth, or it could turn out to be a financial flop. Everything listed, as well as every other possible outcome is fruit- and it is none of my business.

---

73 Thomas Merton, *New Seeds of Contemplation*, 216.

The very thesis of this book- FINOYB- is something I've had to practice while writing it. My reason for writing this book has ultimately landed on obedience to Jesus, so what you do with it is between you and God. I hope you're changed by it, but to be frank, I did my part. I have nothing to prove and no one to impress here. This book's popularity, and how much you're encouraged or transformed by the pages you've journeyed through, is entirely in God's hands.

Lastly, I bet some of you are wired to strategically find the best and most efficient method to achieve whatever you're hoping to accomplish in life. Maybe you've been interested in John 15 or the idea of abiding for some time now. Maybe you've bought other books on the topic, or talked to spiritual mentors about the issue. The problem, however, is that acquiring a mass of information doesn't make you experienced in anything.

I've read from multiple authors a similar message regarding growing a craft or skillset. "You want to be a great gardener? Go garden." "You want to be a great pray-er? Go pray." "You want to make great specialty coffee. Go make coffee." One does not become proficient at something by merely reading more about it. Competence in any area of life grows because of practice. *Consequently, if you want to become a great abider, go abide.*

Moreover, many people are searching for tips and shortcuts to make abiding easier so they can enjoy fruit faster. Once again though, the good things in life take time, and they require hard work and devotion. If you want to experience good fruit for the rest of your life, I give you two suggestions: *firstly, become someone radically defined by abiding in Christ; and secondly, don't forget the first suggestion.*

The abiding life will be one of the greatest challenges of your pilgrimage, but I promise it will be worth it. Make it your aim each day you wake to confess to yourself and to God that you want to root your identity in him, be intimate with him, and be obedient to him. Ask him for help in these, and then attempt with all your strength to abide well, knowing only grace will allow you to be successful.

To sum it up, this whole thing is about intimacy with Jesus. While there are wrong ways to do intimacy with God, there is no right way. I've experienced intimacy with God to be something incredibly ambiguous, and grey, and mystical, and confusing, but this is what particularly strips us of control in the relationship. In time we will be comforted by this reality because intimacy with God is not learned alone. We have the help of the Spirit as we wander. And as J.R.R. Tolkien so eloquently conveyed, not all those who wander are lost.

I want to re-acknowledge what I believe to be the cornerstone to this entire conversation on John 15: *the love of God in Christ Jesus*. After all my "church experience," two degrees, my pastoral training, and ministry experience, I should know a lot of things, but I am only confident of a few things. These are literally the only four things I would bet the farm on: *there is a God, I am not him, his name is Jesus, and he loves us beyond comprehension.*

If you've invested enough time to read this book from cover to cover and nothing landed, I hope this point does: *nothing else in this world can satisfy like the love of God in Christ Jesus.* The love in which Christ calls his followers to abide is an all-consuming love; one that gives meaning, and color, and flavor, and scent to all we experience. No matter your upbringing, no matter your age, no matter your political, doctrinal, philosophical, or ethical beliefs, the love of God is fervently pursuing your heart today.

You are the one Jesus loves; the beloved of Christ. He does not love you for your potential. He does not love you merely because of what he can accomplish through you. He is ruthlessly enamored by you. Passionately in like with you. You are honored sons, cherished daughters of a tender and affectionately good Father. And he loves you not because you are lovely, but because he is. *In the end, your entire life is finally and entirely about your response to the love of God for you in Jesus.*

I pray now that as you close the pages of this book, your heart, mind, will, and spirit would be transformed more readily into the likeness of Jesus; and as you lean into the abiding life, you would bear magnificent, delectable fruit that gives glory to our God and Father in heaven.

"I am the true vine, and My Father is the vinedresser.
Every branch in Me that does not bear fruit He takes away;
and every branch that bears fruit,
He prunes it so that it may bear more fruit.
You are already clean because of the word
which I have spoken to you. Abide in Me, and I in you.
As the branch cannot bear fruit of itself
unless it abides in the vine,
so neither can you unless you abide in Me.
I am the vine, you are the branches;
he who abides in Me and I in him, he bears much fruit,
for apart from Me you can do nothing.
If anyone does not abide in Me, he is thrown away as a branch
and dries up; and they gather them,
and cast them into the fire and they are burned.
If you abide in Me, and My words abide in you,
ask whatever you wish and it will be done for you.
My Father is glorified by this, that you bear much fruit,
and so prove to be My disciples.
Just as the Father has loved Me,
I have also loved you; abide in My love.
If you keep My commandments, you will abide in My love;
just as I have kept My Father's commandments
and abide in His love.
These things I have spoken to you
so that My joy may be in you,
and that your joy may be made full."
JOHN 15:1-11 (NASB)

WORKS CITED

Bourgeault, Cynthia. *Centering Prayer and Inner Awakening.* Lanham, MD: Cowley Publications, 2004.

Bonhoeffer, Dietrich. *Life Together: The Classic Exploration of Faith in Community*, New York, NY: HarperCollins Publishers, 1954.

Brother Lawrence. *The Practice of the Presence of God*, translated by Robert J. Edmonson, Brewster, MA: The Community of Jesus Inc., 1985.

Collins, Jim. *Good To Great.* New York, NY: HarperCollins Publishers, 2001.

Crabb, Larry. *SoulTalk: The Language God Longs For Us To Speak.* Nashville, TN: Integrity, 2003.

Foster, Richard J. *Streams of Living Water: Essential Practices from the Six Great Traditions of Christian Faith.* New York, NY: HarperCollins Publishers, 1998.

Hybels, Bill. *Just Walk Across the Room: Simple Steps Pointing People to Faith*, Grand Rapids, MI: Zondervan, 2006.

Keating, Thomas. *Intimacy With God: An Introduction To Centering Prayer*. Snowmass, CO: Crossroad Publishing Company, 1994, 2009.

Keating, Thomas. *Open Mind, Open Heart*. New York, NY: Continuum International Publishing Group, 1986, 1992, 2006.

Manning, Brennan. *Abba's Child: The Cry of the Heart for Intimate Belonging*. Colorado Springs, CO: NavPress, 1994, 2002.

Manning, Brennan. *The Rabbi's Heartbeat*. Colorado Springs, CO: NavPress, 2003.

Manning, Brennan. *Ruthless Trust: The Ragamuffin's Path to God*. New York, NY: HarperCollins Publishers, 2000.

Manning, Brennan. *The Signature of Jesus: A Path to Living a Life of Holy Passion and Unreasonable Faith*. Colorado Springs, CO: Mulnomah Books, 1988, 1992, 1996.

Menninger, William A. *The Loving Search for God: Contemplative Prayer and The Cloud of Unknowing*. New York, NY: Continuum International Publishing Group, 1994.

Merton, Thomas. *New Seeds of Contemplation*. New York: Abbey of Gethsemani, Inc., 1961, 2007.

Mulholland, M. Robert Jr. *The Deeper Journey: The Spirituality of Discovering Your True Self*. Downers Grove, IL: InterVarsity Press, 2006.

Mulholland, M. Robert Jr. *Invitation To A Journey: A Road Map for Spiritual Formation*. Downers Grove, IL: InterVarsity Press, 1993.

Pennington, M. Basil. *Daily We Touch Him*. Garden City, N.Y.: Doubleday, 1977.

Peterson, Eugene H. *A Long Obedience in the Same Direction: Discipleship in an Instant Society*. Downers Grove, IL: InterVarsity Press, 1980.

Teresa of Avila. *The Collected Works of St. Teresa of Avila: Volume 2- The Way of Perfection, Meditation on the Song of Songs, and The Interior Castle*. Washington, D.C.: ICS Publications, 1980.

Thomas, Gary. *Sacred Marriage*. Grand Rapids, MI: Zondervan, 2000.

Tozer, A.W. *The Pursuit of God*. Camp Hill, PA: Christian Publications Inc., 1982.

Unknown Author, *The Cloud of Unknowing*. New York, NY: HarperCollins Publishers, 1981.

Webber, Robert E. *The Divine Embrace: Recovering the Passionate Spiritual Life*, Grand Rapids, MI.: Baker Books, 2006.

Willard Dallas, *The Divine Conspiracy: Rediscovering Our Hidden Life In God*. New York, NY: HarperCollins, 1997.

Willard, Dallas. *The Great Omission: Reclaiming Jesus's Essential Teachings on Discipleship*. New York, NY: HarperCollins, 2006.

Willard, Dallas. *Renovation of the Heart: Putting on the Character of Christ*. Colorado Springs, CO: NavPress, 2002.

Made in the USA
Las Vegas, NV
23 May 2023

72452470R00121